THE MEDITERRANEAN VALLEYS

GEOLOGICAL CHANGES IN
HISTORICAL TIMES

THE
MEDITERRANEAN
VALLEYS

GEOLOGICAL CHANGES IN
HISTORICAL TIMES

CLAUDIO VITA-FINZI

Lecturer in Geography
University College, London

CAMBRIDGE
AT THE UNIVERSITY PRESS
1969

Published by the Syndics of the Cambridge University Press
Bentley House, 200 Euston Road, London N.W.I
American Branch: 32 East 57th Street, New York, N.Y.10022

Library of Congress Catalogue Card Number: 69-10341

Standard Book Number: 521 07355 3

Printed in Great Britain
at the University Printing House, Cambridge
(Brooke Crutchley, University Printer)

La durée d'un âge historique, d'une étape de la civilisation humaine est négligeable pour le géologue, imperceptible ride sur l'océan des âges.

BERTHELOT, 1927, p. 85

CONTENTS

vii

ACKNOWLEDGEMENTS

This book is based on field-work which I carried out during my tenure of a State Studentship and, later, a Research Fellowship at St John's College, Cambridge, and which was made possible by grants from the Royal Society, the Nuffield Foundation, the Craven and H. A. Thomas Funds (administered by the Faculty Board of Classics, Cambridge), and the Royal Geographical Society. I am grateful to all these bodies for their support.

The field trips were marked by the tolerance and cordiality of almost everyone I met. That they should have proved fruitful is largely due to the advice and wisdom of those I consulted. My greatest debt is to Lady Olwen Brogan and Dr Richard Hey, who introduced me to Libya and taught me in the course of journeys in North Africa what field archaeology and geology I know.

In Tripolitania I benefited repeatedly from the hospitality and professional help of Sig. Mario Fabbri, Mr and Mrs C. H. Johnston, Mr W. Marshall, Mr John H. Stewart, Mr and Mrs H. W. Underhill, the late Dott. E. Vergara Caffarelli, and numerous experts, oil geologists, bureaucrats and tribesmen. The Department of Antiquities allowed me to stay long periods at Lepcis Magna; the Libyan Public Development and Stabilization Agency and the Société Grenobloise d'Études et d'Applications Hydrauliques gave me permission to quote from their reports on Wadis Caam and Megenin. Equally benevolent were the late Dr R. G. Goodchild, in Cyrenaica; Mrs Crystal Bennett, Miss Diana Kirkbride, and Père Roland de Vaux, O.P., in Jordan, the late M. Aymé and MM. Capot-Rey, and Salama in Algeria; M. Souville in Morocco; and Mr B. W. Sparks, Dr E. H. Willis, Mr E. S. Higgs and Dr C. B. M. McBurney in Cambridge. In Italy the changes that interest me, long familiar to Mr J. B. Ward Perkins, had recently been investigated by Dr Sheldon Judson, and he made it easy for me to follow in his footsteps. Dr M. Bradfield, Dr R. U. Cooke and Dr D. R. Harris made many helpful comments on the text. Many of the figures were redrawn by Mrs Mary Hayward, Mr Trevor Allen, and other members of the Cartographic Unit of University College, London.

INTRODUCTION

This is an attempt to discover how far the Mediterranean streams have modified their valleys in the course of the last two thousand years.

The Ancients were well aware that the shape of the land was constantly changing[1] and that this was due only in part to earthquakes and volcanoes: deltas grew, rivers changed their courses, coastlines receded, and mountains crumbled, too weak (as Lucretius put it)[2] to bear the mighty force of time finite. If we consider the last two millennia, the work of the more flamboyant geological agencies is well documented; the eruptions of Vesuvius, like the earth movements that submerged the temple of Serapis at Pozzuoli only to raise it again,[3] have become textbook fodder. The effects of weather, gravity and running water, though less parochial, are duller, and, unless an ancient harbour has been choked by silt or a city buried by mud, they tend to be overlooked.

To assume that the physical landscape has remained essentially unchanged since Antiquity may be justifiable when identifying the landmarks known to Odysseus[4] or in trying to recapture the setting that inspired certain ancient lyrics,[5] for the promontories and mountains are unlikely to have changed beyond the limits of poetic accuracy. But is it safe to go beyond this and conclude, as Myres did with regard to the Aegean,[6] that the physical features and the main possibilities of human livelihood have remained on the whole the same?

Among geologists, interest in the historical period was perhaps greater in the nineteenth century than it is today. In 1818, for example, a prize was offered by the Royal Society of Göttingen for the best investigation into changes in the earth's configuration which could be reconstructed from historical evidence (*quae documentis ex ipsa historia petitis demonstrari possunt*) and their significance in the interpretation of earlier geological events (*ad explicationem longe antiquiorum conversionum...quales planetam nostrum inde a prima ejus formatione pridem subisse testatur quidem geologia*);[7] and it was won by K. E. A. von Hoff with a work filled (in Lyell's words) 'with facts like tables of statistics .[8] Lyell's own

---

[1] See chapter I in Forbes (1963), VII ('Ancient Geology'); Semple (1931), pp. 105–9; Tozer (1897), pp. 184–200.

[2] Lucretius, *De rerum natura*, v, 314–15 (tr. W. H. D. Rouse, Loeb, London, 1966, p. 363).

[3] A view of the temple serves as a frontispiece to vol. I of Lyell (1872); its vicissitudes are described in vol. II, pp. 164–79.

[4] See, for example, Samuel Butler (1897).

[5] E.g. Highet (1959), p. 97, with reference to the springs of the Clitunno, a tributary of the Tiber, described by Propertius and Virgil.

[6] Myres (1953), p. 13.   [7] Von Hoff (1822–41), I, xiii.

[8] Lyell, letter to G. J. P. Scrope (14 June 1830) quoted by Chorley, Dunn & Beckinsale (1964), I, 144.

Principles of Geology, especially in its later editions, is rich in instances of geological changes effected during the span of recorded history.[1] But, once the predominantly gradual nature of geological change had been accepted, the amount of space devoted to the geology of the historical period shrank to a proportion almost commensurate with its share of geological time. Its place has been taken by the writings of those who have sought to expose the evils of man-induced soil erosion, and, more recently, by studies of current processes and their rate of operation. The former are polemical and often pervaded by a sense

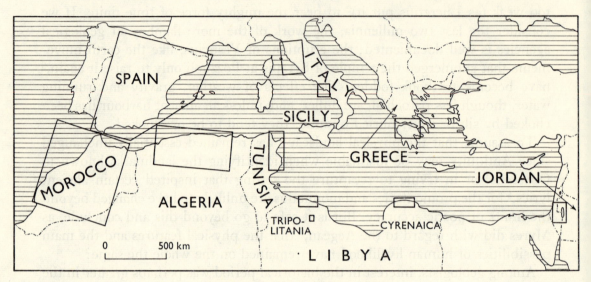

Fig. 1. Areas discussed in the text.

of guilt, while the scope of the latter is limited to the period of instrumental record.

Of greatest relevance to the historian of the Mediterranean world are those changes that have occurred in river valleys, for it is here that agricultural land, water, settlement sites, and routes have always been concentrated. This has facilitated the setting up of geological chronologies, since artifacts can be used to date alluvial deposits and former erosion surfaces.[2] As it happens the present study stems from my chance discovery of Roman potsherds in the banks of a Tripolitanian wadi within a deposit to which I would otherwise have ascribed (by analogy with similar formations in the area) an age of some 30,000 years. Ancient dams, cisterns, and entire (albeit ruined) cities were later to provide a similar service.

[1] Lyell (1872).
[2] Oakley (1964), p. 137. Cf. Harroy (1949), p. 105, who found this approach unsatisfactory in the study of soil erosion.

2

The valleys considered lie within the areas shown on Fig. 1. The wadis of Tripolitania, the first to be studied, eventually yielded a consistent story. The question that next arose was whether it also applied to the rest of the Mediterranean basin. Other workers had identified alluvial formations of historical age in Italy, Algeria and Morocco. I was able to supplement their findings, and to find analogous deposits in Tunisia, Cyrenaica, Jordan, Spain and Greece. What had at first seemed to be a local curiosity was now revealed to be a series of events which had drastically modified the physiography, and, in consequence, the economic potential, of the Mediterranean area since Classical times.

Part I of this book contains the tangible evidence for geological change. The background facts of geology, climate, geography and vegetation have been kept to a minimum in order to avoid giving a pyramidal account with a vast borrowed base and a minute original top;[1] they can easily be filled out with the texts indicated in the references.[2]

Part II is a review of the factors that could have contributed to the observed changes. It reflects all too strongly the major problem one faces in studying the geology of the historical period: how to isolate the effects of human activity on the nature and rate of erosion and deposition.

NOTES

1. The transliteration of Arabic place-names has been enriched by international scholarship to the extent of making consistency impossible. I have therefore adopted the renderings which seem least bizarre. I also use the generic *wadi* (for *oued*, *uadi*, etc.) throughout. It should be noted that this term does not invariably mean that the stream is seasonal; in Palestine, for example, both *wadi* and *nahr* (river) are used for ephemeral and perennial watercourses.

2. The depth of water in some of the streams surveyed sometimes made it impossible to determine the height of terraces above the valley bottom. The figures given in the text must be regarded as minima.

3. The dating of potsherds, particularly if they are water-worn, requires skilled knowledge, experience, and the use of all senses. The authorities who undertook to identify the 'fossil' sherds collected in the course of this study were often handicapped by the absence of a local dated type-sequence. Hence, although some of the sherds were unmistakably of Roman, Greek, Punic or Nabatean age, others could only be subdivided into 'Neolithic' and 'historical' categories. A few were simply sherds. My frequent use of the term 'Classical' in its broader sense of 'pertaining to Greek and Roman times' reflects this difficulty.

[1] Cf. review of Cary (1949) by Sherwin-Whyte (1949).

[2] For general accounts of the Mediterranean, see Semple (1931), esp. ch. VI; Houston (1964) and references cited therein on p. 725; Birot & Dresch (1953 and 1956); Despois & Raynal (1967).

PART I

PART I

CHAPTER I

NORTHERN TRIPOLITANIA

In northern Tripolitania—the starting-point of this investigation—the geologist's task is facilitated by a scanty vegetational cover, which favours the use of air photographs in reconnaissance, and by a deeply eroded topography, which provides excellent exposures for stratigraphic work. These advantages can be exploited in the study of the recent past thanks to a wealth of prehistoric and historical remains with which to supplement conventional geological techniques in the dating of deposits and landforms.

The Tripolitanian Gebel (Fig. 2), a line of hills carved from the northern edge of a plateau which slopes south to the desert, curves eastward from the Tunisian border near Dehibat to the sea at Homs.[1] To the east, it fades into the barren Sirtica. To the north, it is separated from the Mediterranean by the Gefara, a dune-sprinkled plain.

The Gebel, which rises above 800 m in the Garian Massif, lies below 500 m in the plateau country near Tarhuna and the subdued hills occupied by the Msellata tribe around Cussabat. These uplands form a Mediterranean enclave in the sub-desert of the North African coast.[2] The annual precipitation between Garian and Homs ranges from 200 to 350mm, but most of it falls in the course of a few hours in winter[3] and tends to run to waste in violent floods; hot southerly winds and long droughts are a further reminder that altitude does not fully compensate for latitude. The irrigated coastal oases and wadi gardens of the eastern Gebel are luxuriant, and some impressive olive groves and tree plantations have been established, but, apart from these, there is much bare ground and only a sparse cover of grasses and low shrubs, with a few trees[4] punctuating the wadi beds.

The Gebel consists mainly of sedimentary rocks of Mesozoic age,[5] among which limestones predominate. The Miocene, which underlies much of the Gefara, is exposed only in the east.[6] Southeast of Garian extensive basalt flows overlie the plateau and form tongues within some of the wadis that breach the

---

[1] General accounts of the Gebel are given in many of the works cited below. For the western Gebel, see Despois (1935).

[2] UNESCO-FAO (1963), p. 26.

[3] Fantoli (1952), pp. 276, 304.

[4] Franchetti (1914), pp. 203–47; Rowland (1945); Dra (1955), pp. 156–8; Marshall (1960).

[5] For bibliography, see Christie (1955), Magnier (1963), Hecht, Fürst & Klitzsch (1964), and Lexique (1960).   [6] Floridia (1939); COTHA (1956a), p. 9.

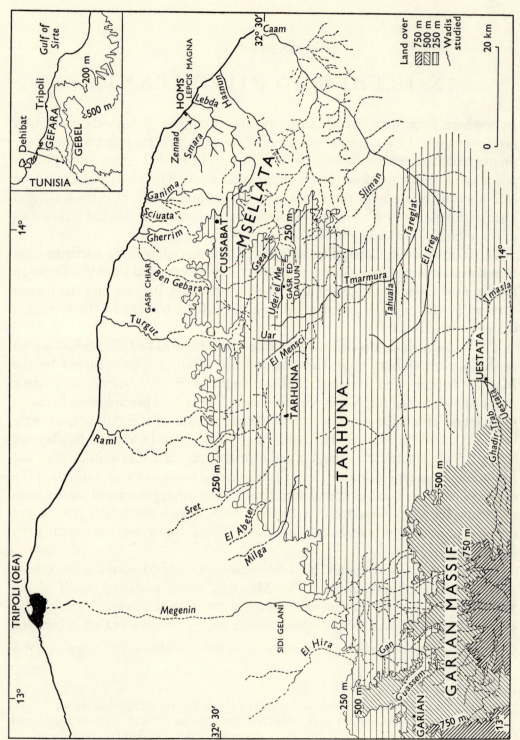

Fig. 2. Location map: the eastern Gebel of Tripolitania.

escarpment. Christie ascribed them to the late Pliocene or early Quaternary,[1] but one of the tongues in Wadi Gan lies within a mudflow deposit thought by Hey to be of late Pleistocene age.[2]

Wind-deposited material, younger than the Wadi Gan mudflow, covers large areas of the plateau, and reaches a thickness of 10 m east of Garian. It consists of angular quartz grains about 0·1 mm in diameter, coated with a film of iron oxide. This 'pink silt'[3] could well be the reddish sandy soil described by Herodotus.[4]

Water erosion has redeposited some of it in the wadis and in the Gefara. The resulting fills and terraces provide most of the information from which the events of the late Quaternary have been reconstructed.

The older valley fill

The first phase of wadi filling may already have started while wind deposition was still operating on the plateau. Aeolian material, which in the early stages of deposition was mixed with poorly-rounded gravel, was laid down by running water to depths ranging from 50 m in Wadi Gan to 1–2 m in the smaller valleys. Where the wadis debouch from the Gebel the surface of this fill is continued by the Gefara, which slopes gently seaward (Pl. 1). Evidence from boreholes led Hey to conclude that much of the sediment underlying the Gefara accumulated during the low sea-level of the Last Glaciation.[5] Within the Gebel a similar date is implied by the presence in the valley fill of Middle Palaeolithic implements; in Wadi Gan they belong to the Aterian,[6] an industry which first appeared in the Maghreb over 30,000 years ago and which was supplanted by Upper Palaeolithic assemblages 15,000 years ago[7] or perhaps even later.

It is difficult to give a general date for the close of deposition. In several wadis the surface of the fill is strewn with late Palaeolithic and Neolithic artifacts;[8] in Wadi El Mensci they include microliths associated with the teeth of a large bovine, probably *Bos primigenius*.[9] Such open finds are of little value in geological dating because they could have been weathered out of the fill. More informative is a slope deposit banked against the Aterian valley fill in Wadi Gan which has buried an apparently undisturbed Intergetulo-Neolithic site.[10] In McBurney's

[1] Christie (1955), p. 21.

[2] Hey (1962), p. 441.

[3] *Ibid.* p. 442. This grade is classed as 'very coarse silt' in Udden's scale, although other authorities regard it as 'very fine sand' (Pettijohn, 1957, pp. 18–19).

[4] Herodotus II, 10–12, quoted by Forbes (1963), p. 23.

[5] Hey (1962), p. 444.

[6] McBurney & Hey (1955), pp. 225–9; Hey (1962), p. 442.

[7] Oakley (1964), pp. 192, 203.   [8] Hey (1962), p. 442.   [9] Identified by Mr E. S. Higgs.

[10] McBurney & Hey (1955), p. 229.

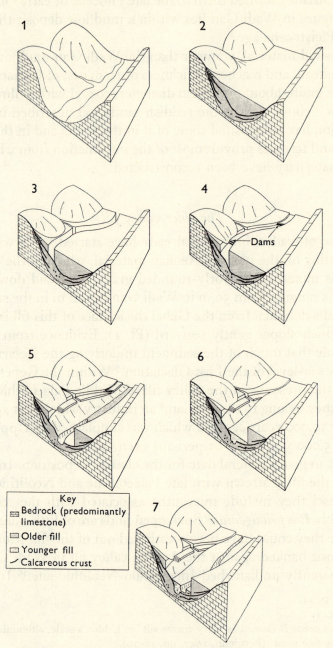

Fig. 3. Schematic block diagrams showing the geological
history of a Tripolitanian wadi.

view this industry is the immediate predecessor of the local Neolithic, and is 'allied to a localised version of the Capsian, or perhaps the Upper Capsian', for which the earliest date in the Maghreb is 6800 B.C.[1] At this site, then, some erosion of the valley fill had already taken place about 9,000 years ago. As will be seen later, Roman remains in Wadi Lebda show that in parts of that valley erosion of the fill had barely begun 2,000 years ago (see Fig. 16).

The fill is rich in calcite and gypsum, and in places is strongly cemented by them. Some of the resulting indurated horizons in the Gefara deposits are several metres thick.[2] Calcareous crusts also occur on the slopes and interfluves, where they cover rock fragments and bedrock. As in other parts of North Africa no single mode of formation can explain all the various types of crust that are present in Tripolitania. Some may have formed at depth, later to be exposed by erosion of the overlying material, as has been suggested with reference to the Sirtic area.[3] Others may represent surface enrichment nourished by capillary rise through the underlying alluvium. Many are best explained by surface deposition from lime-rich waters running off in sheets,[4] for they have a laminar structure, closely follow underlying irregularities such as rock-cut channels or even the surface of individual pebbles, and extend uninterruptedly over the junction between bedrock and valley fill (Fig. 3 (2)).

Lime-enrichment, like the admixture of gravel, decreased in importance as valley aggradation progressed. Hence the upper part of the fill is relatively unconsolidated. Once erosion had supplanted deposition, the watercourses cut steep-sided trenches until they encountered a resistant and extensive crust (Fig. 3 (3)). If its surface sloped across the axis of drainage, the channel tended to shift downslope by sapping the overlying alluvium. If the crust was thin and underlain by poorly cemented material, it was breached. At the Gebel front the wadis have cut through several successive crusts and thus acquired a stepped longitudinal profile. In Wadi Megenin a staircase of this kind starts at a 'water-fall' about 2 km south of Sidi Gelani; Wadi Hasnun descends some 25 m in a series of abrupt steps 3 km above its mouth; and two *gheltas* (the local name for the steps) account for most of the 75 m fall in the lower 10 km of Wadi Turgut (Fig. 4). The headwalls of the *gheltas* retreat upvalley whenever floodwaters gnaw at the alluvium under the hardpan.

By Roman times some of the wadis had migrated to positions approximating to the axes of the original valleys (Fig. 3 (4)); others still flowed over the low cols and hills that had been buried by the fill. The erection of dams within the channels interfered with their development, but this complication is more than

---

[1] McBurney (1960), p. 222.   [2] Willimott (1960), p. 37.

[3] Moseley (1965).   [4] Durand (1959), pp. 12–16.

offset by the value of the dams as reference points against which to measure subsequent erosion and deposition, and as guides to the hydrological conditions prevailing at the time they were in use.

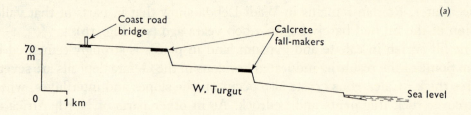

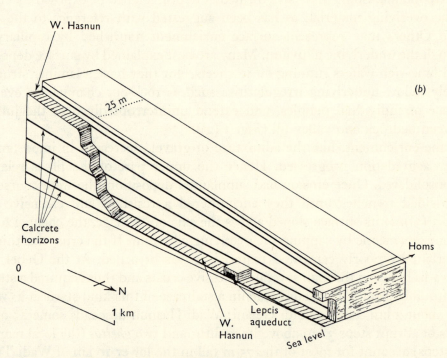

Fig. 4. Longitudinal stream profiles controlled by calcrete horizons:
(a) Wadi Turgut, (b) Wadi Hasnun.

Roman dams

The ruins of ancient dams are found throughout the lands that border the eastern and southern Mediterranean. In date they range from the third millennium B.C. to the late Middle Ages,[1] in function from the storage of drinking

---

[1] Murray (1955), pp. 171–4; Goblot (1963), p. 516.

water to gold-washing.[1] The many Roman dams of Algeria and Tunisia formed part of irrigation schemes; the thorough if not always reliable surveys that were devoted to them at the turn of the century[2] provided massive support for the growing conviction that 'la prospérité de l'Afrique ne fut pas une question de météorologie; elle était le prix du travail'.[3]

Tripolitania is also rich in Roman dams. The first travellers to report on its antiquities were more concerned with the remains of farms, olive presses, forts and monumental tombs.[4] When Italian observers were sent out to investigate the potential of the newly acquired colony[5] the need for water conservation became apparent. In 1929 Badoglio asked for a comprehensive survey of ancient dams to be carried out,[6] doubtless a logical preliminary to the Fascist resuscitation of the Roman Empire in Africa.

The Tripolitanian dams usually consist of a core of rubble and gravel bonded with lime mortar, faced with limestone blocks or carefully laid cobbles, and heavily plastered. The style of construction varies greatly from dam to dam, and sometimes even from one end of the structure to the other, but never to the detriment of robustness. These ancient barrages provide a durable internal cast of the stream channel at the time they were built (provided it can be shown that the intention had been to block the wadi completely) and, if the catchment boasts more than one dam, they give some indication of changes in the stream's longitudinal profile. Furthermore, sediments trapped by the dams provide some clue to the nature of stream flow in Roman times. But first it is clearly essential to establish the age of the dams as closely as possible.

The relevant information is largely circumstantial. Tripolitania lacks anything to compare with the thousands of Himyaritic inscriptions that refer to irrigation in southern Arabia from 700 B.C. into the present era.[7] Even Lepcis Magna, a town with a magnificent water-supply system which involved at least one dam, and the port for an area rich in barrages and other hydraulic works, boasts only two inscriptions which appear relevant, one of them fragmentary and the other obscure.

Writing in the latter part of the first century A.D., Frontinus referred to the

---

[1] As at 'Ainuna in Arabia (Philby, 1957, p. 233).

[2] Gsell (1902); La Blanchère (1897); Gauckler (1897), and criticisms by Despois (1955), p. 45. The assumption that these dams are Roman is sometimes unfounded (Charles-Picard, 1959, p. 41).

[3] La Blanchère (1897), p. 34, quoted with approval by Baradez (1949), p. 172.

[4] Barth (1857) briefly mentioned three dams in Wadi Dauun. See also Cowper (1897), who, incidentally, thought the olive-press uprights were megaliths.

[5] Parona (1913), vol. I, *passim*; Franchetti (1914), pp. 142–6.

[6] Vincenzo Varriale, *I Romani in Tripolitania*, undated MS at R. Istituto Agronomico d'Oltremare, Florence. The survey has hitherto not come to light.

[7] Bowen and Albright (1958), p. 43.

construction of dams as an African tradition.[1] It is likely that the Carthaginians conserved floodwaters by means of small barrages in order to supplement springs, wells and cisterns for irrigation.[2] But the success of their large-scale olive cultivation depended on dry-farming techniques, and it was these which the Romans chose to imitate when Tripolitania came under their direct control in A.D. 69; indeed, the Senate went so far as to decree the translation of the Carthaginian Mago's agricultural handbook into Latin at government expense.[3] By the second century A.D. the entire eastern Gebel from Tarhuna to the sea was densely occupied by olive farms; there is also evidence for extensive plantations in the neighbourhood of Oea and Sabratha.[4] Crops other than the olive, though feasible without irrigation, would give an assured yield only in soils not subject to the whims of rain and flood. Such soils could be provided by diverting freshets on to suitable land, or by damming the streams so that silt was deposited to transform what had been irregular, rocky channels into well-watered, cultivable fields. This undertaking was expensive. The dams thus emerge as more a concomitant than a prerequisite of agricultural prosperity in Tripolitania, and, in the absence of more precise information, this means assigning their construction to the first three centuries A.D.

There is, of course, the possibility that the dams were subsidized or even wholly financed by the State. This would not necessarily conflict with the date proposed in the previous paragraph. It is unlikely that land improvement preceded Roman occupation; air photographs of Tripolitania show very little trace of the rectangular centuriation that indelibly marked Tunisia[5] when the land was surveyed prior to planned settlement. There is some epigraphic evidence for Imperial domains in various parts of Tripolitania,[6] so that the larger dams may have formed part of official projects; but apparently none to substantiate Huntington's suggestion that a decline in rainfall after A.D. 80 prompted the Emperor Nerva and his successors to initiate irrigation works in North Africa as part of their efforts to supply food to Italy and the Empire.[7] What is certain is that, to ensure success, dams had to be built at several points in the

[1] *De controversiis agrorum* II, quoted by Oates (1953), p. 89 n. 9.

[2] Strabo, *Geog.* XVII, 3, 18 (tr. H. C. Jones; Loeb ed., 1932), speaks of 'a kind of cross-wall which the Carthaginans built, wishing to bridge over some gorges which extend up into the interior'.

[3] Pliny, *Nat. Hist.* XVIII, v. 22–3. The work was also translated into Greek by Cassius Dionysius of Utica. (I am indebted to Professor K. D. White for this information.)

[4] Haynes (1955), p. 51. The apparent concentration of dams in the eastern Gebel, doubtless exaggerated by my uneven exploration, was largely the product of early settlement and favourable physical conditions.

[5] See Bradford (1957), pp. 193–207. The exception is a small area near Lepcis (Goodchild, 1949, p. 38).

[6] Reynolds & Ward Perkins (1952), pp. 9–10, and Vita-Finzi & Brogan (1967).

[7] Huntington (1919), p. 204.

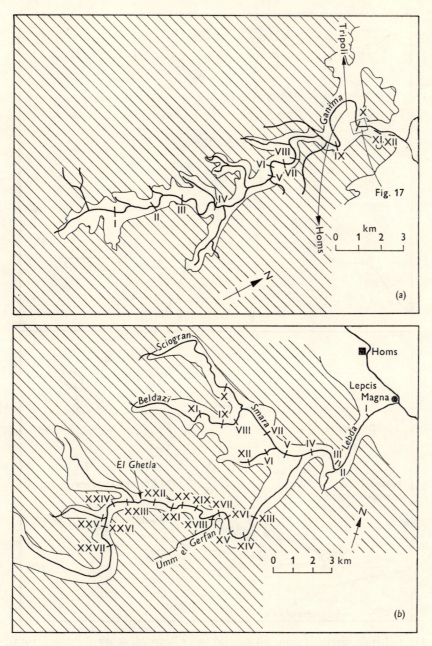

Fig. 5. Location of Roman dams: (a) Wadi Ganima, (b) Wadi Lebda.

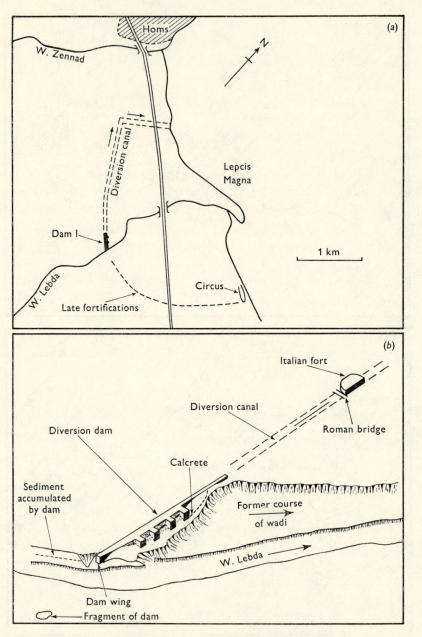

Fig. 6. Lepcis diversion dam: (*a*) location (after Reynolds & Ward Perkins, 1952);
(*b*) view based on an air photograph by the author.

various drainage basins, for otherwise the spates could not be fully controlled. In the Lebda catchment, for example, there are at least twenty-six dams, in the Udei El Me and its tributaries about sixty,[1] and in Wadi Ganima a dozen (Fig. 5). Roman farmers had always formed associations;[2] the *Lex Manciana*, passed under Vespasian, specifically encouraged them to co-operate in such matters as the control of water resources.[3] Furthermore, direct control by Rome over works carried out by provincial corporations in various parts of the Empire became more marked during the second century A.D., whereupon certain major works were carried out by forced labour[4] and by the legions,[5] otherwise condemned to build amphitheatres in Africa (it has been said) for the sake of something to do. The Third Legion came to Tripolitania when Augustus created the Senatorial province of Africa from Numidia and Africa Vetus (which included Carthaginian Tripolis); it did not number more than 13,000 men even with its auxiliaries,[6] but it may at least have provided engineers to plan and co-ordinate private schemes, as they did elsewhere in Africa.[7]

Not all the dams were built to conserve soil and water. Two of them served the special needs of Lepcis Magna. The first, a buttressed dam about 7 m high, 133 m long and 7·25 m thick at the base, deflected the waters of Wadi Lebda along a canal into the sea west of Lepcis[8] (Fig. 6), and so kept its harbour free from silt. It was primarily, if not solely, a protective measure; what has been described as a canal which led the diverted waters towards the northeast for irrigation has turned out to be a low embankment forming part of the city's Byzantine fortifications.[9] One of the inscriptions from Lepcis may refer to the collapse of the dam:

> ...]sin[...
> ...]nis impetu[...
> ...]tatum e[...
> ...]AEDUC[...

[1] Surveyed in 1950 by Messrs R. M. Bradfield and A. Wells.

[2] Rostovtseff (1957), p. 327.

[3] Charles-Picard (1959), p. 64.

[4] Cf. the use of compulsory labour in building water installations in the Negev (Reifenberg, 1953, p. 385).

[5] Choisy (1873), pp. 294–5. According to Tacitus (*Ann.* XI, 20, quoted by Haywood, 1937, p. 52), the *fossa corbulonis* was undertaken to keep troops employed. Legionary recruits made improvements on the Cyrene–Apollonia road in A.D. 100 (Goodchild, 1959, p. 79), and Sapor, the second Sassanid Shah, may have used some of the 70,000 Roman troops he captured in A.D. 26, to build three great bridge-dams with movable sluice gates at Chouchtar, Dizfoul, and Paipol (Goblot, 1963, p. 517).

[6] Charles-Picard (1959), p. 7.

[7] ILS 5795. Cited by Herschel (1899), p. 179.

[8] Romanelli (1925), p. 72.

[9] Goodchild & Ward Perkins (1953), p. 42.

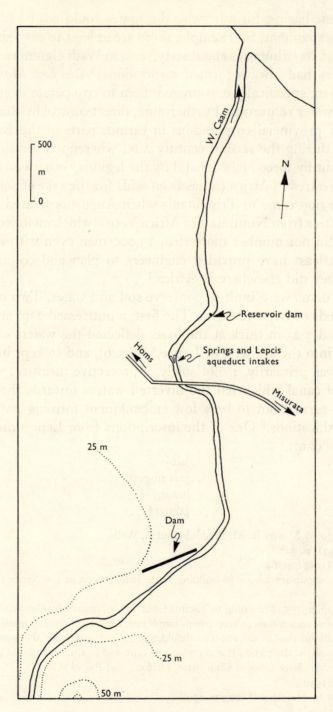

Fig. 7. Sketch-map of lower Wadi Caam.

Fluminis impetu and *aquaeductus* have been suggested[1] for the second and fourth
lines; an aqueduct did indeed run along the wadi floor downstream of the Lepcis
dam. The inscription is ascribed to the fourth century A.D., a plausible date for
the collapse of the dam.[2] As it is known to have been built before the Hadrianic
Baths at Lepcis,[3] it is the most accurately dated dam in Tripolitania.

The second lies in Wadi Caam, 19 km east of Lepcis (Fig. 7). The city drew

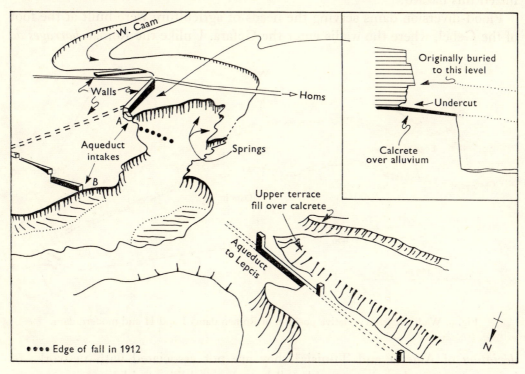

Fig. 8. View of aqueduct intakes and other ancient works in lower Caam.
Inset: detail of wall undercut by flow over calcrete.

part of its water supply from this wadi by means of an underground aqueduct
whose course is marked by a line of *spiramina* or manholes, and which crosses
the floor of Wadi Hasnun 2 km above its mouth (Fig. 4*b*). Immediately upstream
of the intake for the aqueduct, springs flow copiously at the foot of a *ghelta*;
below this point, Wadi Caam is from time to time invaded by the sea: hence its
undeserved reputation as a perennial river. In order to exclude sea water from
this natural reservoir and also to raise the spring waters to the level of the intakes
(a height barely sufficient for the aqueduct to function) a dam 11 m high was

[1] Reynolds & Ward Perkins (1952), p. 186. (IRT 769.)
[2] Cf. Haynes (1955), p. 59.　　　[3] Goodchild & Ward Perkins (1953), p. 45.

built ½ km further downstream.[1] An inscription from Lepcis dated to A.D. 119[2] may refer to this arrangement, as it mentions a new source of water which required raising: 'Q[uintus] Servi[l]ius Candidus sua impensa aquam quaesit[a]m et elevatam in coloniam perduxit.' The numerous other walls near the springs (Fig. 8) ensured that the silt banks did not slump into the reservoir; they also deflected flood waters from it, although other dams further up the wadi minimized this hazard.

Flood-diversion dams serving the needs of agriculture were built at the foot of the Gebel, where the wadis enter the Gefara. Unlike the Roman *barrages de*

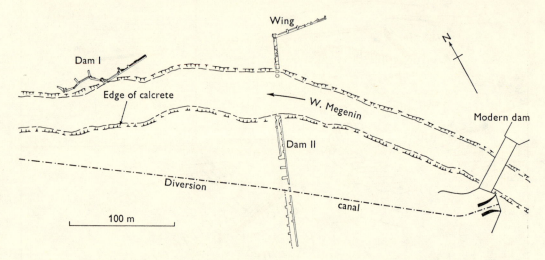

Fig. 9. Wadi Megenin: relative position of Roman dams I and II and modern dam.

déviation of Algeria and Tunisia[3] they are not associated with networks of irrigation canals, but these could well have been obliterated by erosion.

Three notable examples are found in Wadi Megenin. In recent years there have been various attempts to stem its violent spates both to protect Tripoli from flooding and to irrigate part of the Gefara; one of them (in 1955) involved the construction of a diversion dam at the foot of Sidi Gelani, a small hill close to the wadi. This is the obvious site for a barrage that requires anchoring to bedrock, and had already been selected by Roman engineers; in fact the modern diversion canal was laboriously cut through one of the Roman dams.

All three dams are stepped and buttressed, and are equipped with spillways at various levels. Dam II (Fig. 9) consisted of a main wall 210 m long (of which

---

[1] Vita-Finzi (1961), pp. 16–17.
[2] IRT 357. Romanelli (1925), p. 141, thought the reference was to wells.
[3] See above p. 13, n. 2

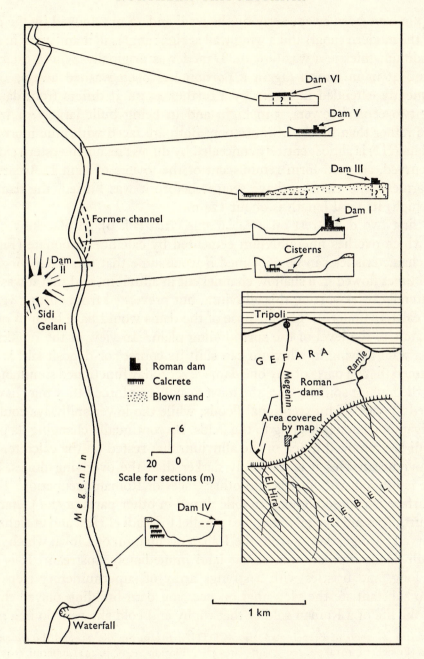

Fig. 10. Wadi Megenin: cross-sections at Roman dam sites.

over 43 m have been swept away by the wadi and 12 m removed by the excavation of the modern canal) and a wing wall at right angles to it and 47 m in length; its maximum thickness was 6·65 m. Dam I was originally 2·60 m thick at the base and 46 m in length (again a portion has been washed away), and was subsequently extended in stages by a further 45 m. It differs from dam II in having two central towers, 5 m high, and in being built largely of well-laid cobbles rather than blocks of limestone. Both are faced with lime mortar. The third dam (III) is almost entirely concealed by dunes; its northwestern extremity has a curved, stepped form reminiscent of the towers of dam I. According to local farmers who claim to have seen it before it was buried, the dam stood 3–4 m high; its total length is about 124 m.

The first two dams rest on a calcareous crust (Pl. 6), in places over 30 cm thick, which overlies fine alluvium cemented by calcium carbonate (Fig. 10).[1] Their characteristics can be explained if we assume that the Wadi Megenin of Roman times flowed in a shallow channel cut in alluvium, and that it was free to shift laterally by re-sorting this alluvium, but prevented from cutting vertically by the calcrete under it. The purpose of the dams would have been to raise the floodwaters to the level of the surrounding plain.[2] In view of the rapidity with which a wadi flowing in alluvium can shift its course[3] or deposit silt, it cannot be assumed that all parts of any one dam we see today functioned simultaneously. But as the highest spillways are the most heavily reinforced they may have been intended to cope with exceptional floods, while the lower spillways could have fed irrigation channels leading to the fields. By continually changing its position the wadi has removed much of the alluvium that rested on the calcrete. Where the alluvium survives it is markedly darker than the overlying dunes, and its surface is littered with sherds and other traces of Roman occupation. This old land surface is exposed among mobile dunes in other parts of the Gefara.[4]

A fourth Roman diversion dam lies parallel to Wadi el Hira and at right angles to a curved barrage, dating from the Italian occupation of Libya, which ponded the wadi floods over an area of flat land immediately upstream. It is almost 200 m long, and bristles with a strange array of supernumerary steps which seem to substantiate the view that on occasion dam-building played the same role in the life of a Roman soldier that rugby and cold showers do in a modern

---

[1] The *plattier de croûte* of French geologists (COTHA, 1954*a*, pp. 69, 73) and the *crostone* of the Italians (Franchetti, 1914, pp. 120–2 and plates 47–9; Floridia, 1939, p. 24; Lipparini, 1940, p. 268). The $CaCO_3$ content of the crust is 83%; the underlying alluvium contains 45%, at a depth of 5 m 24%, and at a depth of 7 m 13% (COTHA, 1954*a*, p. 70).

[2] A similar explanation is given for the Marib Dam by Bowen & Albright (1958), p. 72, and for the early systems in the Nahal Mamshit (Wadi Kurnub) by Shanan, Tadmor & Evenari (1961), p. 14.

[3] Cf. W. Mellègue in Tunisia (Burollet, 1952–3).

[4] McBurney & Hey (1955), p. 263.

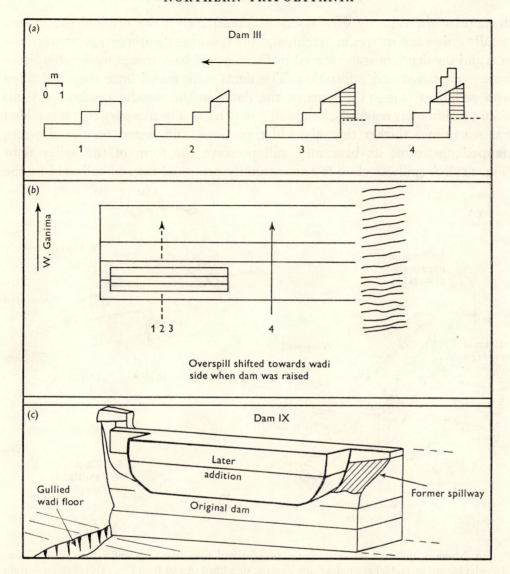

Fig. 11. Wadi Ganima: (a) and (b) section and plan of dam III showing successive stages by which
it was raised after it had silted up; (c) dam IX, showing raised portion shaped to fit the former channel.

army. A dam of similar type is reported from Wadi Raml. Both have spillways
at a level little above the base of the main structure.

Soil-retention was the primary function of the masonry dams built in the
narrow wadis within the eastern Gebel. This was intentional, and not the result
of silting in reservoirs. Oates has shown that many of the dams near Cussabat
(as in other areas) were raised at least once, but always by an amount too small

to increase the capacity of a reservoir significantly;[1] the original dams were usually only a few metres in height, and the resulting disproportion between the area and the depth of water stored by them would have meant intolerable losses from evaporation and infiltration. The dams were raised once they had filled with sediment (Fig. 11); three of the dams in the middle reaches of Wadi Ganima ultimately reached a height of 7 m (Pl. 9).[2] The masonry that was added was sometimes thicker than the older portions, and rested on the alluvium trapped upstream; its base may still preserve the form of the valley floor (Fig. 11c). A spillway close to one extremity protected the soil collected by the

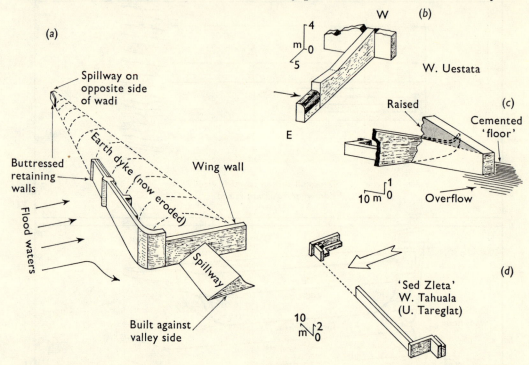

Fig. 12. Masonry spillways for earth dams: (a) idealized case, based on spillway in Wadi Sliman (Tareglat basin); (b) and (c) examples from Uestata, simplified (A and B on Fig. 13); (d) spillway from Wadi Tahuala (Tareglat basin).

next dam downvalley from scour; raising a dam could mean that its spillway had to be moved further towards the valley side.

A modern analogy, though not in Libya, is provided by three earth-fill dams built in the Polacca Wash in the southwestern United States within an arroyo

[1] Oates (1953), pp. 87–9, with reference to dams in Udei el-Me, Gsea and Turgut valleys. Stella (1914), pp. 127–51, is among those who thought the dams were reservoirs.

[2] Depths of 15 or 18 m of silt are thought to have been accumulated by the irrigation systems of the ancient Qatabonians (Bowen & Albright, 1958, p. 4).

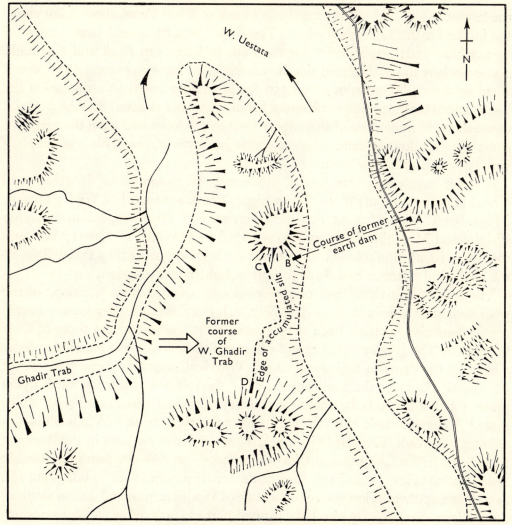

Fig. 13. Wadi Uestata. A, B, C, D: position of spillways.

which had trenched the valley floor to a depth of 10–12 m in the early years of the present century. Since 1944, aggradation has filled the channel above each dam, and practically all the flood flow is used to irrigate the new soils.[1] The reservoirs thus attain their greatest efficiency when filled with sediment; but any water in the Libyan dams would obviously have been a welcome supplement to what could be stored in rock-cut cisterns.

Figures have already been quoted for the number of dams within the Lebda, Udei El Me and Ganima basins. There are at least eight in Wadi Gsea and a similar number in Wadi Dauun. Wadi Tareglat contains several, among them

[1] Peterson & Hadley (1961), p. 189.

the largest known. It stands near the left bank of Wadi Caam about 2 km above the intake for the Lepcis aqueduct. The wadi has torn several large blocks off its northern end; originally it was over 900 m long, 5 m thick and 8 m high. Some workers have suggested that it was intended for water storage and that it silted up after a life-span of about 350 years, a figure based on estimates of the Caam's sediment load (approximately $\frac{1}{2}$ million m³ per annum) and the capacity of the dam (75 million m³).[1] But silt-free water was to be had from the springs a short distance downstream, whereas arable land was scarce. This was simply a very large soil-retention dam.

Another large dam, 6 km farther upstream, was progressively lengthened to a total length of 300 m; it stood 6 m high. Others are found in Wadis Turgut, Milga, Ben Gebara, Uestata, Sciuata, Gherrim, Uar, Guassem, and in the upper El Hira and Megenin. They are also reported from Wadis El Abeter,[2] Sret and the upper Raml.[3] Reference will be made to them whenever they throw light on the geological changes that form the subject of the next section.

The area of cultivable land created obviously depended on the slope of the wadi floor and the height of the dam (Fig. 14). For this reason large watercourses repaid damming, as their beds were generally far less steep than those of their tributaries. The greater violence and volume of their floods was reduced to some degree by the dams in their headwaters. Where all-masonry dams were out of the question because the wadi was too wide, the solution was to use earth dykes protected at both ends by masonry spillways in some cases fitted with sluice gates.[4] A characteristic spillway stands near the right bank of Wadi Sliman, a tributary of Wadi Tareglat (Fig. 12a). There are many others in the Tareglat basin—the fertile Cinyphus of Classical writers[5]—and in the Sofeggin, notably near Uestata (Figs. 12 and 13). One of the structures in Wadi Lebda (dam II), as well as a spillway 6 km above the mouth of Wadi Hasnun and 400 m south of the modern channel, may also have formed part of earth dykes which have since been obliterated.

Stream changes during Roman times

Wherever they are exposed, the foundations of the Roman dams and spillways rest directly on a calcareous crust. This in turn may be underlain by bedrock,

[1] COTHA (1956a), p. 18.   [2] COTHA (1954b), p. 13.
[3] Merighi (1940), II, 77. Also on Geological End Map, Franchetti (1914).
[4] Cf. the dam in Wadi El Hallouf (La Blanchère, 1897, p. 92). Mr J. H. Stewart first drew my attention to the spillways in Wadi Tareglat and to their American-built counterparts. Stone sluices in ancient irrigation systems are reported from Beihân, in the southwest corner of Arabia, by Bowen & Albright (1958), p. 4, and from the Negev by Evenari, Shanan, Tadmor & Aharoni (1961), p. 990.
[5] Herodotus (*Hist.* IV, 198) compared its yields of 300-fold with those of Babylon. Ovid (*Ex Ponto*, II, 7, 25) wrote: *Cinyphiae segetis citius numerabis aristas.*

conglomerate, or poorly consolidated alluvium. Their extremities were not always securely anchored; generally only one end abutted on a bedrock spur, while the other was rooted in alluvium. Erosion of the alluvial fill had progressed enough to expose some good dam sites where two spurs came close together and the valley crust was unbroken. Elsewhere, since one of the banks consisted of incoherent alluvial fill (Fig. 3 (4)), the wadi was free to move laterally. This explains the additions and modifications displayed by many of the Roman dams.

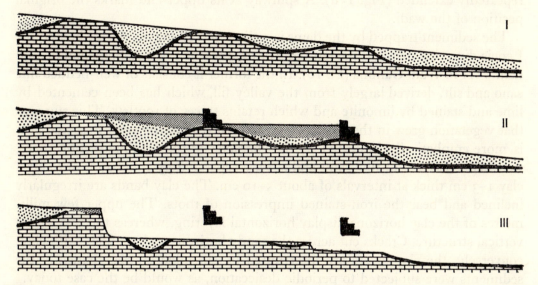

Fig. 14. Wadi profile (I) prior to damming, (II) during the accumulation of soil terraces, and (III) after stream incision has left the dams perched above the wadi floor. Heavy line: calcrete; light stipple: older fill; heavy stipple: dam fill; solid black: dam.

The dams of Wadi Megenin provide an extreme instance. The two largest diversion dams, though only 120 m apart, are at right angles to one another; the wadi runs through the upper dam and along the lower one. Dam I was in all likelihood the first to be built, at a time when this stretch of the wadi flowed at right angles to its present course. The westward additions to the original structure suggest that this was the direction in which the channel was tending to shift; they are increasingly lower and less robust, while the crust on which they rest shows signs of erosion, and they failed to prevent the wadi from cutting its way around the dam. The eastern end was also attacked by floodwaters; some of the blocks of masonry they carried away lie along the line of the former bed, which is clearly visible both on the ground and from the air as it is littered with rounded gravel. Defeat was acknowledged by the construction of a new dam (II) further upstream across the new course of the wadi and solidly rooted in limestone at one end. Although it was provided with spillways, the wing wall of the new dam was probably intended to restrict any further eastward movement of the stream. In this it proved more successful than the extensions to the first dam: the wadi did not change course, but eventually broke straight through the dam.

Dam I in Wadi Ganima illustrates the problems that arose when the calcareous crust that formed the channel floor sloped across the valley. In an effort to keep the dam athwart the stream as this shifted progressively down the crust, it was repeatedly extended (Fig. 15 a). A spillway at its upper end marks the original position of the wadi.

The sediment trapped by the dams is well preserved in two places: behind the Lepcis diversion dam (on the left bank of the present Wadi Lebda), and behind dam VIII in Wadi Ganima (Pl. 10). In the former it consists of well-bedded fine sand and silt, derived largely from the valley fill, which has been cemented by lime and stained by limonite and which retains traces of rootlets. This suggests that vegetation grew in the sediment for at least part of the year. Seasonal flow is more emphatically indicated by the character of the Ganima section; here, well-bedded layers of fine sand and silt are separated by thin bands of reddish clay 1–3 cm thick at intervals of about 5–10 cm. The clay bands are irregularly inclined and bear the iron-stained impression of roots. The upper few millimetres of the clay horizons display horizontal layering, whereas the rest have a vertical structure. Cracks cut across the sandy horizons and are filled with clay; conversely, the clay layers are interrupted by silt-filled cracks. Evidently the sediments were subjected to periodic desiccation, as would be the case today.

Post-Roman changes

De Mathuisieulx had concluded that, in Tripolitania, 'La base des monuments anciens, établis à la lisière des étendues pierreuses, démontre d'ailleurs que le sol est resté exactement au même niveau'.[1] In the valleys, however, important changes took place as a result of continued stream migration and incision after the dams had been broken or circumvented. When all the observed instances are classified, certain general trends in the development of the drainage emerge.[2]

Without constant maintenance the dams were doomed to fail, those that were not anchored in bedrock sooner than the rest. Conditions propitious for neglect set in with the military anarchy that followed the murder of Alexander Severus in A.D. 235. Inflation and grievous taxes afflicted merchants and landowners, and some of the *coloni* who were consequently forced to abandon their lands joined the ranks of the Donatists and pillaged the countryside. This was a foretaste of

[1] De Mathuisieulx (1912), p. 65. [2] Vita-Finzi (1960 a).

the irreparable damage done to the agriculture of the province by the invasions of the Austuriani in 363 and between 393 and 423. In 439 the Vandals crossed to Africa and occupied the coastal areas. The Byzantine re-conquest of Tripolitania was accompanied by further destruction, and did not halt the relapse into nomadic pastoralism. The final blow at settled agriculture was struck by the Arab conquest of 642–3 and driven home by the Hillalian migration of 1050 or 1051.[1] Few dams are likely to have survived long after this.

The wadis continued to change position. In Wadi Megenin, the northernmost of the three flood-spreading dams was left standing 200 m east of the wadi and parallel to it. About $\frac{1}{2}$ km further downstream, in the centre of the channel, stands a wall 43 m long, $1\frac{1}{2}$ m high and 1 m thick, reinforced by seven buttresses and with a rounded top, which rests on the crust lining the wadi floor. Even if it is incomplete, the wall shows that in this reach the wadi had been shallow and had flowed at right angles to its present course (Fig. 10).[2]

The two largest dams in the Tareglat–Caam system have also been abandoned by the stream. As they were both rooted in alluvium, the wadi ultimately found its way around them, not without damaging their masonry. The giant dam now lies along the left bank of the stream. The curved spillway of the second dam is apparently directed towards the south, whereas here Wadi Tareglat flows towards the northeast; its former alignment is marked in the left bank by traces of a buried channel filled with sandy alluvium containing Roman potsherds.

Two of the Wadi Ganima dams, north of the coast road, lie parallel to the modern channel and some distance away from it; the others are still at right angles to the wadi. In Wadi Gherrim, close to the coast road, a small dam lies, like dam V in Wadi Megenin, within the channel but no longer across it.

As Wadi Gsea shifted down its sloping calcareous floor near Bir Bu Summit, it left a large dam standing 20 m away from the modern stream bed (Fig. 15 b).[3] The efforts that were made to prolong the life of dam I on Wadi Ganina have been described; the absence of similar extensions to the Gsea dam, a much more important structure, suggests that it had fallen into disuse before the stream moved to its present position.

The spillway (dam II) which lies on the convex bank 5 km above the mouth of Wadi Lebda (Fig. 16) almost certainly rests on the crust which is exposed in a nearby gully at a depth of 2 m. East of the spillway (Pl. 8) there is a flat-topped terrace of well-rounded gravel which contains rolled potsherds and which rests on the calcrete. The second dam, 250 m to the west, is an all-masonry barrage

---

[1] For a fuller account, see Haynes (1955), pp. 54 ff., and Goodchild (1952b).
[2] The older local inhabitants recall shifts in the course of the wadi during their lifetime.
[3] See Oates (1953), pl. XXIIIc.

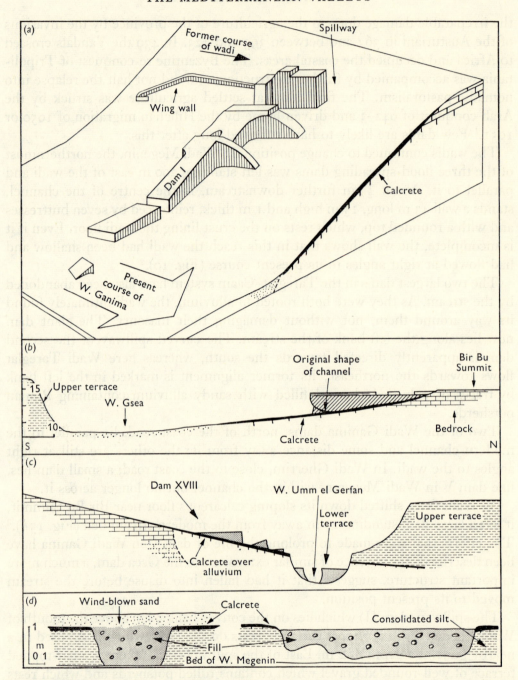

Fig. 15. Calcrete: responsible for downslope shift of stream at (a) dam I, Wadi Ganima, (b) Bir Bu Summit, Wadi Gsea (based on survey by Dr Maitland Bradfield); breached before deposition of post-Classical deposit at (c) dam XVIII, Wadi Lebda, and (d) upstream of modern dam, Sidi Gelani, Wadi Megenin.

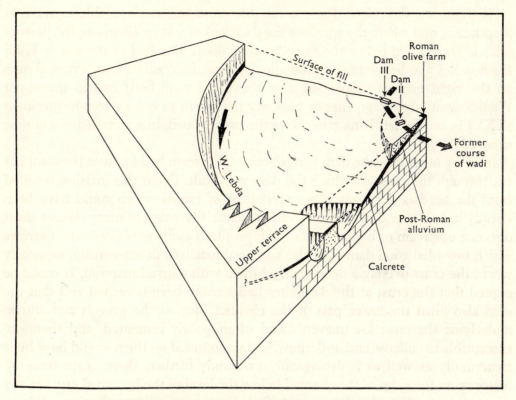

Fig. 16. Wadi Lebda: position of dams II and III, former extent of
older fill, and breached wadi calcrete.

normal to the present course of the wadi. The crust on which it rests dips southwards to the wadi and rises again under the alluvium of the opposite bank (Pl. 7);
the dams are at about the same elevation as the surface of the valley fill. The
wadi must have continued to flow at this level long enough for the dams to be
constructed and for alluvium and gravel to be deposited, before shifting down
the crust. An ancient quarry on the right bank, below the level of the dams and
in limestone that would have been exposed only after the removal of the
Quaternary overburden, shows that some of this shift was accomplished during
Roman times.

Other dams in the Lebda basin illustrate the same point. For instance
dam XIII, which rests on crust-capped bedrock, is now 50 m away from the
stream bed and 5 m above it; the end of dam XV is 25 m from the edge of the
deep modern channel. Aggradation induced by the dams themselves encouraged
stream migration: Wadi Ghadir Trab was displaced northwards and Wadi
Lebda was pushed towards the east for this reason.

At those few dam sites where a suitable crust was not available to serve as foundation, and where the whole of the dam had to rest on alluvium, the present wadi is entrenched below the former valley floor. The bed of the upper Wadi Hasnun lies 3 m below the original alluvial floor; in Wadi Sciuata a ruined dam on the right bank is suspended 4 m above the wadi bed; and in the upper Wadi Snanat large fragments of masonry that seem to belong to a former dam (XXV) lie on the left bank 7 m above the present bed, in which bedrock is now exposed.

In every other case the dam hangs above the stream bed because the wadi has cut through the crust on which the dam was built. Often this incision resulted from the headward retreat of a waterfall or of rapids which could have been already in existence downstream from the dam. The siting of many dams a short distance upstream of breaks in the wadi profile is easily explained; the narrows which provided good dam sites also favoured localized down-cutting, especially where the crust overlay a deep channel filled with alluvial material. It could be argued that the crust at the dam sites had already been breached and that the dam also filled the lower part of the channel. But, as the gravels and alluvia underlying the crust are unevenly and often poorly cemented, and therefore susceptible to collapse and underflow,[1] a dam founded on them would have been structurally as well as hydrologically unsound; further, there is no trace of masonry on the sides of the channel below the level of the breached crust at any of the sites, or of conglomerate or calcified alluvium adhering to the dam masonry that lies on the wadi floor. The base of the dam, when mentally reconstructed from those fragments that remain in place and those that have been broken off, always forms a simple curve that agrees in shape with that of the crust where it is still unbroken; and, with the possible exception of the northern end of dam I on Wadi Megenin, it rests on a surface which shows no signs of erosion.

Several of the dams in Wadi Lebda hang as a result of waterfall retreat. At dam II, where lateral shift over the sloping crust preceded downcutting, the total drop in the level of the wadi was 12 m; at dam XV it amounted to 7·30 m. In other cases the crust was breached directly under the barrage: dam IV is now 4 m above the wadi floor; at dam VI deepening has attained 3 m, at dam VII 2 m and at dam VIII 4 m.

The waterfall, an alcove with a vertical headwall, is usually to one side of the channel (Pl. 2 & 11); the rest of the cross-section is eroded only during major floods. This is the case with the falls that have retreated to about 400 m above

---

[1] Cf. the *sous-écoulement* and *éffondrement* of Hubert (1948). The thirteenth-century dam at Saveh (Iran), though handsome, rested on 'porous' alluvium through which the stream found its way. According to the chronicles, its architect committed suicide (Goblot, 1963, p. 516).

dams IV and VIII. Sometimes two deep cuts have developed at the same section and have isolated 'islands' of conglomerate capped by a crust, as at the foot of dam II.

Elsewhere along the Lebda and its headwaters the crust has been broken through wherever its undulating surface was intersected by the profile of the wadi. In Wadi Snanat just above its junction with Wadi Lebda, an 'anticline' with a core of cemented gravel is neatly exposed in section on the left bank.

In Wadi Caam the headwall above the springs is still being attacked by spring-sapping and by plunge-pool action during floods (Pl. 12). In 1912 the right-bank intake near the road extended for a few metres over a ledge that has since retreated[1] (Fig. 8). Where it is still unbroken the crust successfully restricts stream activity to bank erosion. This has exposed the foundations of one of the walls that lined the eastern side of the Lepcis reservoir.[2]

At Sidi Gelani, Wadi Megenin broke through the crust on which the two large dams rest and then cut down to a maximum depth of 1·80 m (Fig. 10 and Pl. 13) to form a terrace. This extends about 2 km upstream from the dams, and down-stream for 1 km; in this reach gullies are eroding the indurated, nodular alluvium that underlies the crust, which thins out towards the east where it passes under the right bank. The bottom gullies are localized on one or other side of the wadi floor, and, when viewed in conjunction with the evidence of the *gheltas*, suggest that downcutting is effected by the integration of discontinuous gullies along part of the stream bed.

It has long been the practice to conserve some of the floodwaters of Wadi Megenin in cisterns which are excavated in its bed and then capped by a truncated cone of masonry. Some of the cisterns are thought by local farmers to be Roman; others are obviously modern, and new ones continue to be made. Upstream of the Roman dams the supposedly ancient cisterns are found on the crust terrace above the reach of most floods, whereas the modern cisterns stand on the present wadi bed. Downstream, Roman cisterns as well as their recent counterparts stand on the wadi floor, showing that this stretch had been cut below the crust by Roman times.

Further south all that remains of dam IV is its right wing, 6 m above the wadi floor; the canyon head which was responsible for this has retreated a further 800 m. Above it, the wadi floor consists of the uppermost calcareous horizon exposed in the sides of the gorge, and $2\frac{1}{4}$ km further upvalley a small piece of dam is still in place on it. Dam V also lies on the crust which lines the modern wadi bed, but dam VI, which is 26 m long and 1·70 m thick, has been completely buried by deposition in the channel.

[1] De Mathuisieulx (1912), pp. 82, pl. 13.   [2] Butler (1920), p. 69, describes similar effects in Syria.

A few more examples will suffice. A small tributary of Wadi Ganima, at kilometre 90 on the Homs road, has cut through a thick crust overlying gravel and bedrock to leave a small dam perched 7 m above the wadi bed. In Wadi Ben Gabara, ¾ km above the old road from Gasr Chiar to Cussabat, a dam hangs 2 m above the wadi on the left bank; in Wadi Milga and the Udei El Me many of the dams hang by about 1 m for the same reason.

The younger valley fill

In addition to the main terrace of redeposited aeolian material, Hey had observed in many of the larger wadis of the Eastern Gebel a second lower terrace containing larger and more abundant pebbles.[1] It occurs in a fragmentary state in almost every watercourse, however small (Pls. 3, 4).

The fines in this terraced fill consist almost entirely of subangular quartz grains identical with those of the earlier Quaternary deposits; 50–80 per cent by weight are retained by the 200 sieve, and the rest is silt with some clay. About half of the sand grains have lost their coating of iron oxide, probably by reduction during or after deposition. They are well bedded, and the stratification is emphasized by fragments of mollusc shell.

The gravel is almost entirely of limestone with occasional basalt pebbles; some of it is subangular and some well rounded. In the samples taken this depends on pebble size, those between 5 and 10 mm in diameter showing the best rounding. Contrasts in the smoothness or pitting of the surface of the pebbles are often entirely due to lithological differences. Sorting is poor; scattered boulders over 1 m in diameter may occur (Pl. 5) and the maximum gravel size bears little relation to channel dimensions. Gravel and silt are more clearly segregated than in the older fill. Even so, the gravel is by no means 'clean', and its poor sorting and high content of interstitial material suggests deposition by floodwaters.[2] These characteristics are echoed by the sharp boundaries between poorly sorted gravel patches and areas of fines on the modern stream floor.[3]

Sherds were to be found at all levels in this terrace in every wadi except Wadi Gan, and most plentifully in the Msellata, where a long history of dense settlement has strewn the ground thickly with pottery. Their presence helps to identify fragments of the lower terrace which are so eroded that they cannot be distinguished visually from remnants of the higher terrace. Wheel-turned pottery was not in common use in Tripolitania before the arrival of the Romans;[4] most of

[1] Hey (1962), p. 442.　　　　　　　　　[2] Pettijohn (1957), pp. 288 and 541.
[3] Cf. Chaco Canyon fill in Bryan (1954), p. 25.　　[4] Haynes (1955), p. 20.

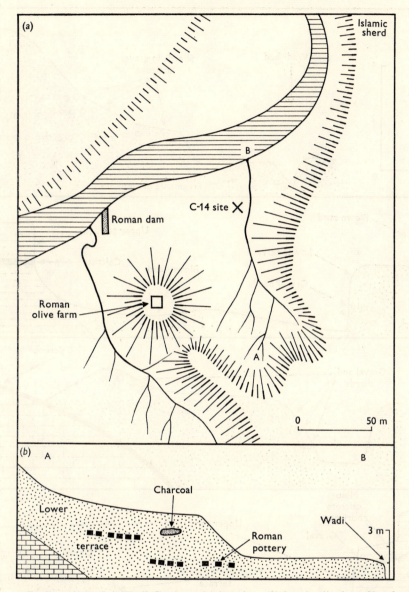

Fig. 17. Radiocarbon site, Wadi Ganima: (a) location, (b) longitudinal profile of gully.

the sherds in the terrace are of coarse reddish ware, and are thought to date from the first century B.C. onwards.[1] Two rolled Neolithic blades in the lower terrace in Wadi Lebda and a disc scraper from that in Wadi Hasnun provide cautionary examples of the erroneous dates that incomplete searching can give; found

[1] According to Sig. M. Fabbri of the Department of Antiquities, Tripoli.

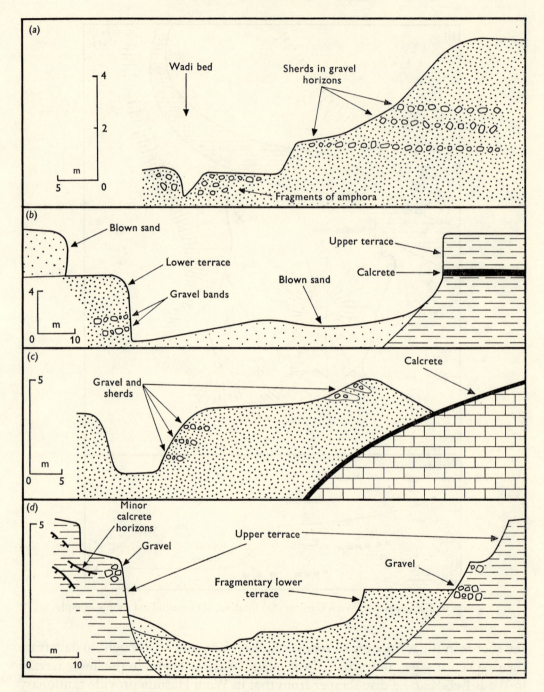

Fig. 18. The younger fill: (a) still in course of incision, lower Wadi Zennad; (b) within a channel cut into the older fill, Wadi Turgut; (c) middle Wadi Zennad; (d) upper Wadi Hasnun.

alone, they might have recruited a new adherent to the cause of a Neolithic Pluvial in North Africa.

A single green sherd of Islamic type in the upper part of the terrace in Wadi Ganima implies a medieval date for at least the later stages of deposition. In the middle of the same terrace 200 m further upstream, a lens of charcoal, exposed by a gully (Fig. 17), has given a radiocarbon date of 610±100 B.P.[1] This places the mid-point of deposition in the fourteenth century, a slight improvement on the term 'medieval'.

The fill lies in channels cut into the older wadi deposits (Fig. 3 (6), 18 b, d).

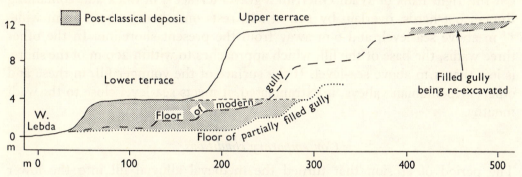

Fig. 19. Wadi Lebda: post-Classical deposit filling lower and upper parts of a gully cut into the older fill.

Their erosion supplied much of its material. The maximum depth of deposition was 10 m. The height of the lower terrace obviously depends on how deeply the streams have cut into the fill, so that there is no obvious correlation between terrace height and the size of the wadi. The width of the terrace depends on the size of both the modern channel and that in which it lies; at one point in the lower Wadi Snanat it exceeds 40 m, for deposition on the outside of a convex bend kept pace with erosion of the upper terrace on the opposite bank.

The medieval deposit was laid down both in the lower parts and at the heads of gullies which trenched the older fill (Fig. 19). Thus 2 km south of Lepcis Magna, on the upper terrace, gullies 2 m deep were filled with alluvium and rubble partly derived from a nearby Roman site, and their mouths were invaded by the younger fill of Wadi Lebda. Where they are not filled, these 'old' gullies can look deceptively fresh.[2]

In several reaches where the wadi crust had survived unbroken until Roman times, it was breached by the time the younger fill was laid down. In Wadi Megenin, a short distance upstream of dam II, gullies were cut into the cal-

[1] (Lab. No. Q-656) Grid ref. 321450 on Tripoli 1/100,000 map, Fondugh En-Naggaza and Homs sheet (Vita-Finzi, 1963).   [2] Cf. Leopold & Miller (1954), pp. 79–80.

careous alluvium under the crust and then filled with gravel containing Roman pottery (Fig. 15*d*). In Wadi Umm El Gerfan, a southern tributary of Wadi Snanat, the lower terrace lies in a channel cut through the crust on which dam XVIII rests (Fig. 15*c* and Pl. 14). Large blocks of dam masonry are found within the younger fill in Wadis Hasnun, Tareglat, Ganima and Lebda.

Drifting sand obscures the geology at the mouths of wadis that boast fine terraces in their middle and upper reaches. In only four of them could the younger fill be observed close to the shore—Gherrim, Ganima, and two unnamed wadis east of the latter—and even here its relationship to sea-level was not clear. On the right bank of Wadi Gherrim a gravel terrace $\frac{1}{2}$ m thick and containing Roman potsherds, overlain by 1 m of silt, rests on a bench about 10 m wide, $1\frac{1}{2}$ m above sea-level, and 6 m away from the present shoreline. In the other three wadis, the base of the fill, which approaches to within 200 m of the shore, is less than 1 m above sea-level. If the surface of the younger fill, in these and other Tripolitanian valleys, is extrapolated, it meets sea-level close to the wadi mouths.

Contemporary conditions

The period of erosion that turned the medieval alluvial fill into the lower terrace is still active. In some reaches—as in the middle Zennad—the wadis have not yet cut down to the base of the fill (Fig. 18*a*); everywhere the terraces are being consumed by bank sapping, downcutting and gullying. The first two processes operate during spates, some of which originate from rainstorms higher up the catchment basin, while gullying can act only if local rains are sufficiently protracted or intense for runoff over the alluvium to take place.

The gullies are either short, fairly evenly spaced and at right angles to the parent wadi (Pl. 16), or linked in dendritic networks. They have stepped, discontinuous longitudinal profiles.[1] Their heads advance rapidly: footpaths are cut and fields destroyed.

Once the crust has been breached (Pl. 15), the undulating bed of the main wadis is replaced by a stepped profile resembling that of the gullies (Fig. 20). The breaks retreat by sapping and by underflow; the profile increasingly reflects hydraulic factors, although the surviving crusts still limit the freedom of this adjustment. Wadi Lebda epitomizes this trend.[2]

Sometimes the development of a new profile is effected by deposition. Where active lateral gullies enter the main wadi, they spread flat cones of alluvium across the floor. Similarly, aggradation characterizes the lower reaches of most of the major wadis. We have already seen that dam VI on Wadi Megenin was

[1] Leopold & Miller (1956), pp. 29–33. [2] Vita-Finzi (1960*b*).

buried by silt; the wadi currently deposits large quantities of sand just south of Tripoli at each flood.[1] The Roman cisterns in Wadi Lebda, which were excavated by Italian archaeologists, have been buried again by about 3 m of alluvium. The floods of 1955–6 in Wadi Caam led to aggradation in all the observed reaches.[2]

Aggradation at the lower end of the treads in the stepped longitudinal wadi

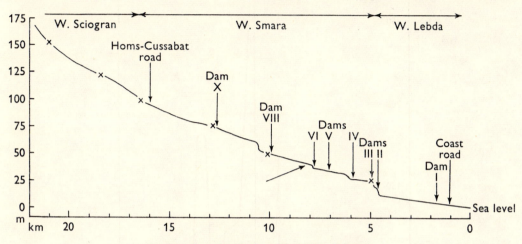

Fig. 20. Longitudinal profile of Wadi Lebda.

profiles contributes to the flattening effect achieved by sapping at their heads. Each of the treads itself has a discontinuous profile; the gravel patches on the valley floor often lie immediately upstream of gully heads which are attacking the wadi bed.

The floods that produce these changes are rare and shortlived (Fig. 21). The only discharge records available are those for Wadi Caam during the period 1954–7:[3]

Year	Total annual discharge (in million m³)	Peak discharge (in m³/sec)	Number of floods	Duration of longest flood
1954–5	9·5	160	8	32 hours
1955–6	15·5	310	9	3 days
1956–7	15·2	155	9	2 days

The coefficient of discharge, that is the proportion of the rainfall that runs off in the streams, is low. For example, the Caam basin received 228 million m³ in 1954–5 and 330 in 1955–6, so that the respective coefficients were 0·042 and 0·047. Much of the water is lost by infiltration and evaporation, even though the most intense downpours come in autumn when runoff is encouraged by the

[1] Stewart (1956).　　　　　　[2] COTHA (1956b), p. 5 and fig. 4.
[3] COTHA (1956a), pp. 2–3; (1956b); (1957).

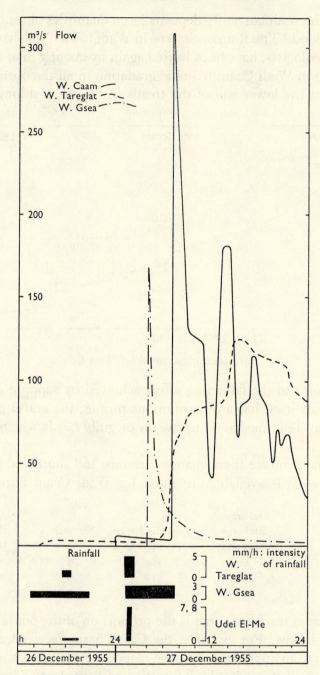

Fig. 21. 26–27 December 1955: (*a*) flood discharge, and (*b*) intensity and duration
of rainfall, in three parts of the Tareglat basin.

paucity of vegetation after the summer drought, and raindrop impact can form an impermeable surface on fine-grained alluvium. But it should be borne in mind that the Tripolitanian rains may be given a deceptive air of intensity by the large size of the raindrops.[1] In fact, a rate of 0·1 mm per minute is rarely exceeded, whereas 12 mm per hour (giving an average of 0·2 mm per minute) is apparently not an extraordinary occurrence in Italy.[2] While it may occasionally happen that half the annual mean falls in one day,[3] rains totalling over 20 mm are rare: in Tripoli (with an annual mean total of 370·8 mm), they account for 8·8 per cent of the rainy periods,[4] or about fifty rainy days in the year.

Even so, the brief rains produce floods whose hydrographs have very sharp peaks (Fig. 21). As the rainstorms are usually very localized, a wadi may be undergoing a violent flood while its neighbours or even its tributaries remain completely dry.

In these circumstances it is surprising to find that all the watercourses should today display an overall flattening of gradient, and an increase in the length and number of channels (or drainage density),[5] tendencies similar to those which had characterized the period immediately preceding the deposition of the younger fill.

The southern Gebel

So far we have considered the streams that drain the eastern escarpment of the Gebel. The southern slope of the Gebel escarpment is furrowed by a network of gullies and broad wadis, most of which ultimately unite to flow eastwards into the Gulf of Sirte (Fig. 22). There is a sparse steppe vegetation;[6] the mean annual rainfall fluctuates violently around a mean of 100 mm. These marginal lands on the threshold of the Sahara were largely neglected in the early stages of Roman development,[7] until the reorganization of the southern frontier by Septimius Severus—to some extent in response to tribal unrest—called for the settlement of veterans. This process (which played a vital part in the development of southern Algeria by Trajan)[8] was accelerated under Alexander Severus. The *limitanei* were established mainly in the Zemzem and Sofeggin basins. Exploitation of the land was inevitably patchy,[9] and, when the Third Augustan Legion was disbanded and the frontier was broken up into a number of self-contained zones, agriculture became even more devoted to local needs.

[1] Fantoli (1952), p. 78. [2] *Ibid.* p. 81. [3] *Ibid.* p. 51. [4] *Ibid.* pp. 87, 229.
[5] Horton (1945); Scheidegger (1961), pp. 195–7. [6] For references, see above, p. 7, n. 4.
[7] Goodchild (1950), p. 161. The recent discovery of a Neo-Punic inscription in Wadi Amud, 45 km southeast of Mizda, by Lady Brogan (1965), shows that there, at least, cultivation had begun as early as the first century A.D. [8] Broughton (1929), p. 119.
[9] Goodchild & Ward Perkins (1953), p. 2.

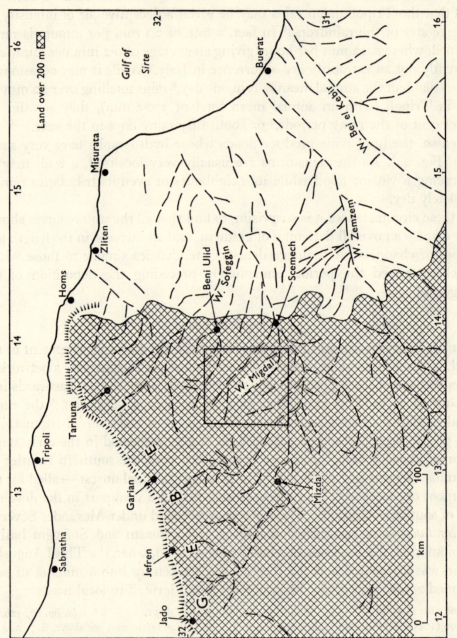

Fig. 22. Southern Tripolitania: position of Wadi Migdal.

Successful cultivation was made possible by the use of dry-stone walls which, though lower than the dams of the eastern Gebel, served a similar purpose in slowing down and spreading the rare spates; like the dams, they were raised once they had filled with alluvium. By collecting the runoff from the surrounding hillsides, the wadi walls at Beni Ulid (which are now again in use) give the wadi bottom for a distance of 10 km the equivalent of 500–600 mm of annual precipation in an area whose mean rainfall is less than 75 mm per annum. With similar rainfall, but without wadi walls, flood-irrigation can ensure a crop two years out of three, and only if the gradient of the wadi bed and the volume and

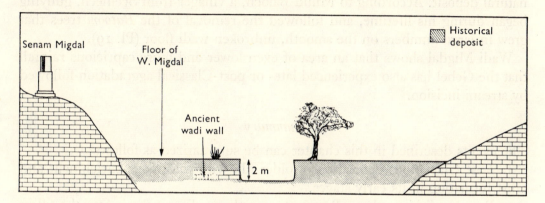

Fig. 23. Cross-section of Wadi Migdal.

speed of the flood remain within certain limits, approximately a slope of $\frac{1}{2}$ per cent for a flood not exceeding 1 m in depth and a speed of 1 m per second.[1] In other words, the chances of success are slim.

By the fourth century the population of this border zone may have exceeded that of the coastal belt.[2] Procopius, writing in the fifth century, says that the water-conservation works in these parts were still *in auge*;[3] and the continued beneficial effect of these walls may account for the renowned fertility of the Sofeggin valley in the eleventh century when El Bekri was writing.[4] Ultimately, sedentary agriculture became restricted to the more favoured wadis while the rest of the population reverted to nomadism.[5]

As it was essential to have datable material available, the investigation had to be limited to wadis within the Roman *limes* and preferably in areas of permanent inhabitation. Wadi Migdal, a tributary of Wadi Sofeggin, yielded useful information.[6] Its floor is interrupted by a large number of partly buried walls composed

[1] Stewart (1960). [2] Goodchild & Ward Perkins (1953), p. 2.
[3] Quoted by Caputo (1951), p. 217. [4] Quoted by Oates (1953), p. 112 n. 43.
[5] Goodchild & Ward Perkins (1949), p. 95.
[6] Lady Brogan had reported gullying of the wadi bed.

of uncemented blocks of limestone. The treads of this alluvial staircase consist of silt that was protected by side walls against runoff fron the rocky slopes.[1]

Valleys over a kilometre wide and with indefinite margins are not suited to the survival of a terrace sequence. Near Senam Migdal, however, a section of the bottom deposits has been exposed by recent gullying (Fig. 23 and Pl. 17). It shows fine alluvium, with a maximum observed thickness of 1·70 m, overlying a system of dry-stone wadi walls which closely resemble the Roman walls found at the surface further upstream (Pl. 18). In this reach no dyke or dam protrudes above the valley floor, and the alluvium that buried the walls appears to be a natural deposit. According to Milud Baloch, a villager from Scemech, gullying began during his lifetime, and followed the removal of the *Batoom* trees that grew in large numbers on the smooth, unbroken wadi floor (Pl. 19).

Wadi Migdal shows that an area of even lower and more capricious rainfall that the Gebel has also experienced late- or post-Classical aggradation followed by stream incision.

Summary

The events described in this chapter can be summarized as follows:

1. Last Glaciation: deposition of older fill, with calcareous enrichment and crust formation in its early stages.

2. Post-Neolithic and pre-Roman times: the wadis cut down into the fill as far as the first major crust, which they breach in a few places.

3. Roman period: dams are erected to accumulate silt; the wadis continue to shift over the crust towards the axes of the valleys originally cut in bedrock.

4. Late Classical period: the crust is breached at many dam sites; drainage density is increased by the development of gullies.

5. Middle Ages: the younger fill is deposited to a maximum depth of 10 m, with a consequent reduction in drainage density.

6. Present day: both fills are eroded; the wadis flatten their longitudinal profiles and gullies once again increase drainage density.

Before this succession can be interpreted, we should consider the evidence from other parts of the Mediterranean.

[1] Goodchild (1950), p. 166.

CHAPTER 2

CYRENAICA

The Gebel Akhdar, or Green Mountain, is a hilly protuberance in the extreme north of Cyrenaica, the eastern province of Libya. Like the Tripolitanian Gebel, it interrupts the sub-desert climate of the North African coast by virtue of its relief.[1]

The Gebel is bounded on the north and west by two main escarpments which are cut through by numerous wadis (Fig. 24). Its maximum elevation approaches 900 m; large areas exceed 500 m. The yearly rainfall, irregular and restricted almost entirely to winter, ranges from 200 to over 650 mm; annual variability at Cyrene may attain 1:13. The character of the rains is not unlike that of Tripolitania, with a similar range of intensities.[2] The cover of Mediterranean vegetation, largely scrub with pine and cypress, is particularly dense on the sides of the northern wadis,[3] and thins out towards the steppe and the desert on the southern slopes of the Gebel. The hills are made up chiefly of Miocene limestones, with some Eocene, Oligocene and Cretaceous rocks, which dip gently southwards.[4] Outcrops of bare limestone separate pockets of red soil.

If one omits coastal dunes, the most important continental Pleistocene deposits are tufas and gravels laid down in the wadis during the Last Glaciation.[5] The tufas were precipitated by springs, in one case (Wadi Derna) to a thickness of 30 m. Then came the accumulation of up to 20 m of 'Younger Gravels' in a *terra rossa* matrix which spread out as fans at the seaward end of the wadis. Both these deposits post-date a period during which sea-level stood at 6 m above its present position.

In many of the Cyrenaican streams, as in Wadi Migdal, stone dykes were built in Classical Antiquity to curb the spates.[6] Unfortunately they have survived only in the upper reaches, where the Younger Gravels or other deposits susceptible to erosion or redeposition are lacking, and they are themselves too low and too weak to serve as geological markers. But potsherds, already reported *in situ* from recent marine deposits at Benghazi,[7] once again helped to date recent alluvial deposits.

Many of the depressions on the plateau are filled with soil, predominantly

---

[1] UNESCO-FAO (1963), p. 26. For a strange amalgam in Latin of ancient and modern accounts of Cyrenaica, see Rainaud (1894).   [2] Fantoli (1952), p. 304 and *passim*.
[3] Higgs (1961), p. 145.   [4] Gregory (1911); Desio (1935); Marchetti (1938); Hey (1956).
[5] McBurney & Hey (1955), pp. 72–129.   [6] Goodchild (1952*a*), (1952*b*), (1959).
[7] Desio (1935), I, 348.

terra rossa. Where it had been exposed by ditches or by trenches dug for pipe-laying (as along the Barce road, southwest of Cyrene), the infill yielded sherds, among them several of Roman type. This suggested that the bulk of the soil had been washed down during or after Roman times. Some of these deposits are now being gullied by the headwaters or tributaries of wadis; in addition true terraces occur within the main valleys. The observations that follow come from five watercourses which drain the northeastern part of the Gebel, Wadis Gla'a, Kuf, Bel Ghadir, En Naga, and Susa, of which the last two contain large perennial springs, respectively 'Ain Mara and 'Ain Susa. They all display a terrace lower than that formed by the Younger Gravels.

In Wadi Gla'a, where it is crossed by the coast road, the deposit is 4 m thick and consists of poorly sorted, rounded gravel and boulders mixed with *terra rossa*, and rich in Roman sherds. The terrace is rendered discontinuous by the irregularity of the underlying bedrock.

In Wadi Bel Ghadir, which notches the escarpment immediately to the west of Cyrene, the depth of fill is the same; but here it forms extensive terraces, sometimes over 30 m wide, and consists of well-stratified horizons of brownish-red earth, fine gravel in a sandy matrix, and coarse gravel. The proximity of Cyrene guaranteed a plentiful supply of pottery; in fact, the terrace is in some places so full of potsherds that it resembles occupation (or excavation) debris. As the sherds at all levels in the formation include both Greek and late Roman types, aggradation cannot have begun before the fourth century A.D. Further, a gravel layer near the top of the formation at the head of the wadi yielded a fragment of green Islamic pottery and three pieces of modern bottle glass, which indicate that deposition in this reach continued into the present century. In confirmation of this, a photograph of the upper wadi in the Archives of the Cyrene Museum, taken in the 1930s, shows that the wadi then had a flat floor which was crossed by a path; today a gully has cut back to a depth of 2 m below this floor.

Wadi Kuf drains the rainiest part of Cyrenaica and flows through a deep gorge amid limestone cliffs riddled with caves. In the reach extending 1 km below and 2 km above the bridge on the main Barce road, the deposit is up to 6 m thick (Pls. 20, 21). Its upper horizons consist chiefly of *terra rossa* which displays little bedding except for occasional pebble bands and lenses of crushed mollusc shells. The base of the deposit contains sub-rounded and poorly sorted gravel, and in turn overlies eroded limestones and conglomerates.

There is generally a distinct shoulder at the junction between the main wadi and its lateral tributaries, so that the terrace is often thinner in them (Fig. 25 b). Here one gains the immediate impression that deposition has filled in a drainage

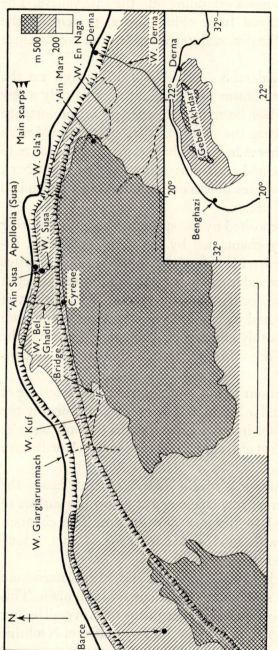

Fig. 24. The Gebel Akhdar, Cyrenaica: location map.

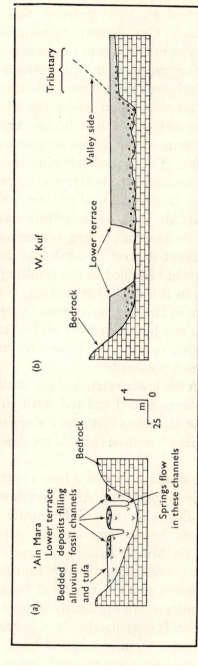

Fig. 25. Cross-sections of (a) Wadi En Naga at 'Ain Mara; (b) Wadi Kuf.

system in which the tributaries did not always join the parent stream accordantly, to produce a flat-topped vale with tongues extending into the side valleys. The material for this operation was derived from older alluvia, principally the Younger Gravels, with the nature of the depositing streams determining whether fines or gravel was to predominate.

The width of the fill varies considerably, and obviously depends on the underlying relief. Where this takes the form of a gorge, it may be only a few metres wide; but, where the wadi has been free to wander, as for instance upstream of the Kuf bridge, or where the entry of a tributary provides an embayment, the terrace on one or other side of the channel may exceed 100 m in width. The gravel contains sherds and also flint artifacts. The right-bank terrace above the bridge also contains three blocks of hewn limestone which had fallen from a classical site above the stream.

At 'Ain Susa, a mass of tufa was deposited by the spring at some stage during the Pleistocene; it was subsequently channelled by the wadi. A bedded, incoherent deposit of earth and gravel with a few thin horizons of tufaceous material has filled in the resulting irregularities to a maximum observed depth of 3 m (Pl. 22). Downstream, it also forms alluvial terraces with a height of $3\frac{1}{2}$ m in two successive reaches separated by a fall of several metres in the wadi bed, and lies on bedrock and on smoothly abraded conglomerate. In colour the deposit ranges from brown to grey according to its tufa content. It contains Roman potsherds.

In the lower reaches of the wadi, about $1\frac{1}{2}$ km south of Susa, a 2 m terrace of boulders, gravel and red earth yielded a Neolithic blade. This is probably the same deposit as that near the spring, for in other Libyan wadis the only terraces to yield Neolithic remains are those that also contain pottery of Greek or Roman age.

A similar situation is found in the upper Wadi En Naga. Near their heads, the copious springs of 'Ain Mara flow in narrow channels cut below the surface of the flat valley floor. They unite a short distance downstream. The channels expose bedded gravels and clays with intercalated horizons of tufa, which contain Middle Palaeolithic implements[1] (Fig. 25a).

A gravelly deposit with thin bands of dark grey silt and with a maximum thickness of $2\frac{1}{2}$ m has filled broad, shallow channels cut into the plain. This material stands out clearly when it is exposed in section owing to its overall lighter colour. It contains sherds of Roman pottery. Microlithic flint blades of Neolithic character occur in a bed of black silty clay lying immediately under the gravel fill, the upper part of which, when sieved, yielded minute fragments of red ware.

[1] McBurney & Hey (1955), pp. 120–3.

As these are certainly post-Neolithic, silt deposition is seen to have continued beyond the Middle Palaeolithic period into historical times, until the channels were cut. About 700 m downstream the fill occurs as a terrace 3 m high composed of rounded limestone pebbles and broken fragments of tufa.

The picture that emerges is one of widespread aggradation in historical times, which at least in one reach did not begin before the fourth century, and in another gave way to downcutting only forty years ago. There is no sign of the stream migration and downcutting that typified post-Roman Tripolitania, but the Younger Gravels and the underlying bedrock did not encourage vagaries of this kind.

CHAPTER 3

TUNISIA

The Lower Tell of Tunisia[1]—the foothills of the High Tell—consists of undulating ground with isolated mountains; most of it lies below 400 m (Fig. 26). Southwards it passes into lowlands that lead into the Tunisian steppes, of which the Sahel, an area of low hills and broad depressions, is the cultivable portion. It receives from 400 to over 700 mm of annual rainfall and is well cultivated; the Sahel has less than 400 mm. Runoff is highly irregular and there is little perennial stream flow,[2] but abundant dew, subsoil water, and low evaporation allow the extensive cultivation of olives. Agricultural development began in Carthaginian times and gained momentum under the Romans.[3] Some of the most striking examples of centuriation known come from the Sahel and Northern Tunisia.[4]

The mountains of the Lower Tell are composed of folded Cretaceous, Eocene Miocene and Pliocene rocks. The Quaternary has contributed calcareous crusts, screes, and alluvial deposits, some of which have been dated archaeologically.[5] As in Tripolitania and in the Dahar of southern Tunisia, the reddish silts that mantle the plateaux pass into alluvial cones at the foot of the escarpments and form a terrace within the wadis which contains Aterian artifacts.[6] A second, less widespread terrace about 2–3 m high in the Dahar wadis has been described as 'submoderne';[7] it also occurs in several valleys between Sfax and Tunis, and contains sherds of Roman pottery.

In Wadi Lakhderi, about 20 km north of Sfax, and in Wadi Djidida, southeast of Grombalia, the terrace has a maximum height of 3 m. In Wadi Boul, 5 km west of Enfidaville, the terrace is again 3 m high and consists of well-bedded gravel, sand and silt; in some places the deposit merely forms the upper metre of the low wadi banks and overlies older alluvium.

Immediately to the northeast of Takrouna, on the margins of the High Tell, a group of gullies which flow into Wadi Brek (Pl. 23), also a short distance west of Enfidaville, reflect a similar story: lime-indurated alluvium at the base of the

---

[1] For general accounts, see Admiralty (1945), pp. 1–42; Despois (1955).
[2] Runoff data in Gosselin (1941), and Despois (1955), pp. 75–87; see also UNESCO-FAO (1963), p. 26. [3] Charles-Picard (1959), pp. 59 ff. [4] Bradford (1957), pp. 193–207.
[5] Castany (1952, 1962); Burollet (1956), pp. 223–40; Coque (1962), pp. 398–9.
[6] Castany (1962), p. 264.
[7] Robaux & Choubert (undated, a), pp. 13–14; Robaux & Choubert (undated, b), pp. 12–13; Robaux & Choubert and others (undated), pp. 14–15.

TUNISIA

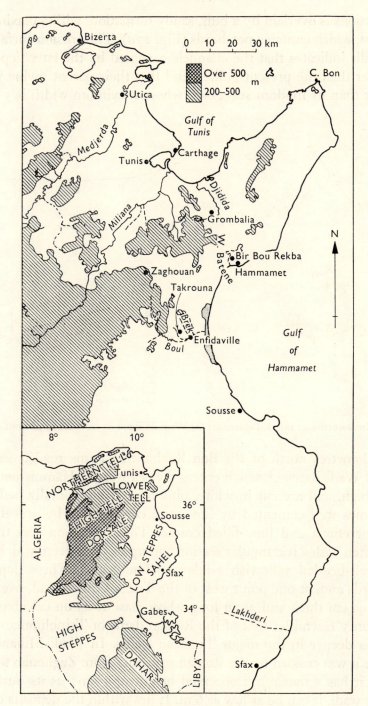

Fig. 26. Eastern Tunisia: location map.

exposed sections is overlain by a buff, sandy formation, with a maximum thickness of $4\frac{1}{2}$ m, which contains potsherds (Fig. 27a). The erosion surface between these two fills indicates that the channels occupied by the later deposit were a little broader than the present gullies, and that their parent ravine was several times wider than its modern successor, whose maximum width is 5 m.

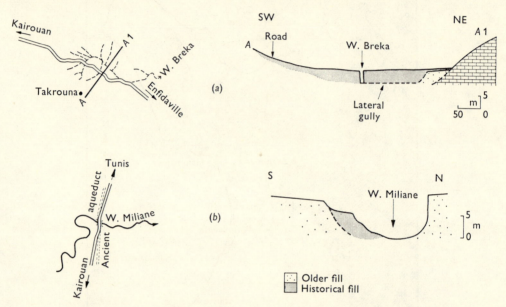

Fig. 27. Cross-sections: (a) at Takrouna; (b) Wadi Miliane at crossing of ancient aqueduct.

Three kilometres north of Bir Bou Rekba, the Tunis road crosses a small tributary of Wadi Batene,[1] which enters the sea west of Hammamet. Its banks are 2–4 m high, and are cut in white, pink or red, horizontally bedded clayey silt, sometimes well cemented by lime, and complicated by gravel beds, calcareous concretions and lime-filled cracks. This formation was trenched by channels, often with a rectangular section and up to $3\frac{1}{2}$ m deep, which were later filled by well-bedded yellowish sands and fine gravel. These deposits yield Roman sherds and, at one point west of the Tunis–Sousse road, overlie a stone wall about 90 cm thick and 20 m long whose base rests on calcareous silt and whose masonry resembles that of the Roman dams of Tripolitania.

The fill is deeper in the major Tunisian wadis. In Wadi Miliane, near the point where it was crossed by the Roman aqueduct from Zaghouan to Carthage[2] (Fig. 27b), it has a maximum observed height of 10 m; as its surface slopes towards the wadi, it can be as low as 6 m. It lies within the deposits of an upper

[1] 1/50,000 map of Tunisia, Sheet xxx (Nabeul), grid ref. 560 × 351.
[2] Sheet xxviii (Bir Mcherga), grid ref. 520,5 × 371,0.

terrace about 20 m high, composed of calcareous alluvium with a high silt content whose bedding is emphasized by colour banding in a series of grey-greens and browns.

Abundant sherds lying on the upper terrace, too numerous to have been weathered from it, suggest that this may have been the land surface in Roman times. The top of the lower terrace forms the floor of lateral gullies cut into the older deposits. As usual the latter fill is predominantly buff or greyish-brown, with gravel at its base and with cross-bedded, sandy horizons. About $\frac{1}{4}$ km downstream of the bridge, a large block of hewn Classical masonry protrudes from the lower terrace.

In the Medjerda, Tunisia's principal stream, recent flood-deposits accumulated by bridges and other obstructions (and in one case containing lemonade bottles and the carcass of a camel) obscure the terrace sequence. But the rapid growth of its delta from early Classical times is noteworthy. The ancient port of Utica is now 12 km from the sea,[1] and had already been abandoned by the seventh century A.D.[2]

The Roman dams of Tunisia, to judge from descriptions given by previous workers, provide some analogies with those in Tripolitania in their relationship to the present natural drainage. For example, Wadi Kastela has been deepened at one point 2 m below the base of a Roman dam,[3] and in Wadi Khemila the foundations of an ancient dam are now 5 m above the level of the wadi bed.[4] Similarly, changes in the position of Wadi Boul made it necessary for a Roman dam to be repeatedly rebuilt, and have left other Roman water-control structures standing above and away from the present channel.[5]

The gullies that served to expose the fill northeast of Takrouna are symptomatic of the erosion that typifies Tunisia no less than other Mediterranean lands, although here it is being fought with unusual zeal.[6] The position of Roman remains in relation to the land surface and to ravine heads led Tixeront to conclude[7] that sheet erosion has been negligible since Roman times, that linear erosion has predominated, and that it has performed most of its work during the last few decades.[8]

[1] Burollet (1952), p. 21.   [2] Admiralty (1945), p. 33.   [3] La Blanchère (1897), p. 48.
[4] Gauckler (1897), p. 92.   [5] La Blanchère (1897), p. 65.
[6] See, for example, Marthelot (1957), Sogreah (1959), Neyrpic (1959).
[7] Tixeront (1951), pp. 76–80.   [8] *Ibid*. Twenty years at the time of his writing.

CHAPTER 4

ALGERIA

The relief of northern Algeria is dominated by the Tertiary folds of the Atlas. In the west the country can be divided into three zones.[1] The Tell Atlas consists of a succession of mountain ranges, plateaux and valleys, with the main lines of the topography roughly parallel to the coast. South of it lie the High Plateaux with its basins of internal drainage (*chotts*) and then the broken ridges of the Saharan Atlas. In the east these divisions are not so clear. The various components of the Tell Atlas merge into one another, while the two main mountain chains are linked by branches, notably the Hodna mountains which separate the High Plateaux from the high plains of Constantine.

The streams that flow into the Mediterranean between Arzew and Cape Bogaroun drain from the Tell Atlas, the High Plateaux and the high plains of Eastern Algeria (Fig. 28). Their catchments receive annual precipitation totals ranging from 300 mm in the south to over 2,000 mm in parts of Kabylie. In most districts the bulk of the rainfall comes in autumn, winter and spring, with a maximum in December and January. In the coastal belt the vegetation, where relatively undisturbed by man, consists of mixed Mediterranean forest and dense scrub; the High Plateaux have a steppe vegetation.

The rocks that outcrop in this area range in age from Archaean and Pre-Cambrian (in the Djurdjura) to Pleistocene (chiefly in the lowlands and on the coast), but Jurassic, Cretaceous and Tertiary beds predominate. The marine and alluvial Quaternary formations attracted early attention, notably De Lamothe's classic studies of raised marine beaches.[2]

In his work on the western Atlas, Anderson[3] described four stages of lateral planation, aggradation, and trenching by streams which followed a period of denudation early in the Pleistocene. Of these, the last two were marked by the deposition of alluvial fills. Anderson named the older of these two fills after Mazouna, his type site; the younger, which was laid down after an intervening period of erosion, he called the Chelif stage as it was particularly well developed in that valley. Two alluvial terraces characterize most wadis in northern Algeria (Pl. 25), and, as they seem to correspond to Anderson's two fills, his nomenclature may be retained.[4]

The Mazouna fill, here taken to include the terraces described by Anderson[5]

---

[1] Admiralty (1943), pp. 27–63; UNESCO-FAO (1963), pp. 25–6.　　[2] De Lamothe (1899).
[3] Anderson (1932).　　[4] Vita-Finzi (1967) and references.　　[5] Anderson (1932).

and the littoral *couches rouges* of French workers, was laid down during the low
sea-level of the Last Glaciation.[1] Its overall red colour is derived from inter-
granular iron oxide and the admixture of *terra rossa*. It contains an Aterian
industry; near the coast, Oranian implements are found within the upper
horizons and on the surface of the *couches rouges*.[2]

The silty deposit into which the lower Isser and Soummam (Pl. 24) have cut
their channels, described by De Lamothe,[3] and the *terrasse récente* which Boulaine

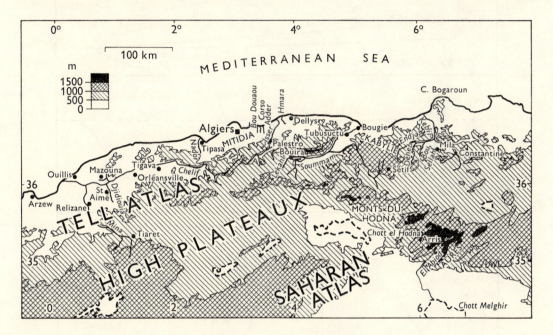

Fig. 28. Northern Algeria: location map.

investigated in the Chelif valley,[4] both correspond to Anderson's Chelif stage
(Fig. 29 *b*, *c*). This formation underlies the floor of all the valleys shown on
Fig. 28, and its surface (except in the case of Wadi El Aboid, which flows into
Chott Melghir) slopes down to meet sea-level at the mouth of the stream
(Fig. 29 *a*).

The Chelif fill rests unconformably on bedrock or on older Quaternary
deposits. There is some broad correspondence between depth of fill and stream
dimensions. For example the deposit attains a maximum thickness of 3 m in
Wadi Corso, 4 m in Wadis Deheb (Pl. 26), Hmara, Bou Douaou and Bou
Sellah, 5 m in Wadis El Abiod, Lekahl and Endja, 6 m in the Mina, and 8 m in

[1] Balout (1955), p. 46; Arambourg (1951), p. 49.
[2] Balout (1955), p. 50; Hilly (1962), p. 361 and n. 1.
[3] De Lamothe (1899), pp. 279–80, 298–9.   [4] Boulaine (1957), pp. 437–44.

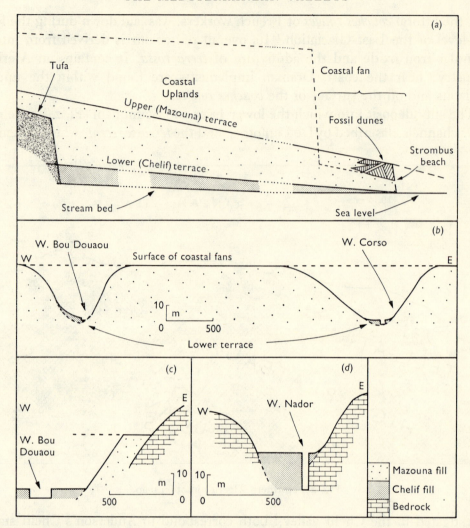

Fig. 29. (a) Idealized longitudinal profile of an Algerian wadi; (b) cross-section of alluvial deposits near the coast (Wadis Corso and Bou Douaou); (c) the two terraces in the middle Bou Douaou; (d) the lower terrace in Wadi Nador, 6 km above its mouth.

the Isser and Chelif valleys. But disproportionate thicknesses occur where the buried surface is unusually irregular: thus the fill is 20 m thick at one point in Wadi Nador[1] (Fig. 29d).

The fill consists of silty fine sand with horizons and lenses of gravel and coarse sand. In general, texture changes abruptly, although some of the gravel bodies grade upwards into fines. The sands are well stratified and sometimes display cross-bedding; they are commonly stained by iron and cemented by calcium

[1] Map of Algeria, Sheet 40 (Tipasa), 1/50,000, grid ref. 473,3 × 361,0.

carbonate. The dominant colours are grey and yellow-buff: the larger the valley the finer and greyer the fill, presumably thanks to prolonged transport and reduction under waterlogged conditions.[1] The gravel, of various sizes, at various stages of rounding, and poorly sorted, is usually concentrated at the base and at the margins of the deposit. The fill contains abundant remains of land snails; freshwater species are uncommon.

In this part of Algeria there are numerous ancient sites on the banks of streams to act as a source of datable material. Extensive areas had come under cultivation during the rule of Massinissa. The first two centuries A.D. saw the steady southward extension of Roman settlement;[2] in the east it reached the Aurès, although the Kabylie Massif and other difficult areas were not effectively occupied. The Chelif fill duly rendered up Punic and Roman sherds at almost every exposure.

As in Tunisia and Tripolitania, Roman dams provide evidence of changes in the form or position of watercourses. According to Gsell, Wadi Mina has cut itself a new channel around a dam near Relizane;[3] in Wadi Khelidj Sakhri a block of masonry 2·50 m thick protrudes from the left bank above the stream bed;[4] and in Wadi Barika part of a large dam 's'est bientôt trouvée suspendue au dessus du vide'.[5] To these examples may be added that of a well-preserved barrage in Wadi Djidiouia, near St Aimé; this has been totally engulfed by the Chelif fill, here up to 10 m thick.

In Wadi Endja, the lower terrace has combined with slope wash to bury the floor of a Roman house now exposed in the stream bank. Debris from the Roman baths of Tigava (modern Wattignies) lies at the base of the fill in the Chelif itself. The lower terrace of Wadi Soummam provided the most satisfactory fossil: part of the Roman town of Tubusuctu, at Tiklat, 3 km southwest of El Kseur, revealed by the floods of December 1957.[6]

The close of a phase of deposition can rarely be given a precise date, as incision tends to progress upstream. Anderson believed that although North Africa had seen 'insignificant changes' during the last two thousand years[7] the Chelif fill was trenched comparatively late, for its surface was little affected by erosion and had received little debris from the surrounding hills;[8] but he conceded that the present streams had already cut down to their former level and in some places were several hundreds of metres wide. According to Boulaine, deposition of the *terrasse récente* of Wadi Chelif began long before the Neolithic period, and gave way to downcutting shortly before historical times; but near Orléansville, where Carthaginian remains are exposed in the river bank, this

---

[1] On significance of red beds, see Van Houten (1961), p. 121.   [2] Warmington (1954), pp. 25–6.
[3] Gsell (1902), p. 42.   [4] *Ibid.* p. 83.   [5] *Ibid.* p. 84.   [6] Lassus (1959), pp. 278–93.
[7] Anderson (1932), p. 866.   [8] Anderson (1936), p. 368.

could not have taken place until the fourth century B.C.[1] The archaeological evidence here described shows that the Chelif phase of aggradation postdates Roman settlement. Stream incision is therefore even more recent; indeed, early in the present century there still lived some locals who could remember when the Chelif cut its channel upstream of Boghari.[2]

The Algerian streams are now widening their beds by sapping their banks, particularly during the winter floods, and extending their courses by erosion at their heads. The density of the drainage network is also being increased by the development of gullies. Modern flood deposits can be distinguished from those of the Chelif fill by their incoherence; they can also be dated archaeologically: witness a gravel terrace in the middle Isser which was found to contain roof tiles stamped with the date of their manufacture in Algiers. They are generally coarser than the Chelif fill, presumably because the violence of peak flood flow is now greater than during its deposition.

[1] Boulaine (1957), pp. 365–6.　　[2] Joly (1940), quoted by Boulaine (1957), p. 436 n. 8.

CHAPTER 5

MOROCCO

The High Atlas of Morocco is the prolongation of the Saharan Atlas of Algeria; between it and the Sahara rises the Anti-Atlas. The Middle Atlas runs north-eastwards to form the main watershed of Morocco, with the Moroccan Meseta between it and the Atlantic coast. To the east lie the High Plateaux of Algeria. In the north of the country the Rif mountains are separated from the Moroccan Meseta by a zone of lowlands.[1]

Unlike the rest of the Maghreb, Morocco has a climate which is dominated mainly by Atlantic influences. In the western and central Rif, the Middle Atlas, parts of the Moroccan Meseta, and locally in the High Atlas, the annual precipita-tion (much of it snow) exceeds 600 mm[2] and supports forests of fir, cedar and evergreen oak; in areas of lower rainfall, *maquis* and steppe associations prevail.

The observations that follow refer to perennial and seasonal streams draining to the Mediterranean, the Atlantic and the Sahara[3] (Fig. 30); their basins consist of rocks of varied lithology which date from the Pre-Cambrian onwards. One of these streams, the Bou Regreg, was the approximate southern limit of the Roman province of Tingitana; Carthaginian, Berber and Arab sites provide archaeological dates for geological features in other parts of the country.

Quaternary geologists have found evidence in Morocco for five pluvials, the Moulouyan, the Saletian, the Amirian, the Tensiftian and the Soltanian, which were followed by the Rharbian (or Gharbian)[4] 'half-cycle'.

The Rharbian deposits are extensively developed in the plain after which they are named, and form the *basse-terrasse* (2–4 m high) of the Moroccan valleys.[5] They are described as being distinctively light in colour, often grey, in contrast with earlier Quaternary formations, which are predominantly red. Gigout has gone so far as to equate greyness with 'freshness'.[6] Their alluvium is fine-grained and free from calcareous crusts,[7] and what little gravel they contain is usually well rounded.[8]

Estimates of the age of the Rharbian sub-phase vary, though always within the limits imposed by the fact that they obviously postdate the Soltanian deposits

---

[1] Admiralty (1941), p. 1; Dresch and others (1952).   [2] UNESCO-FAO (1963), pp. 24–5.
[3] Ambroggi and others (1952); Loup (1960); for a study of longitudinal profiles see Célérier & Charton (1924).
[4] Anglicized version, e.g. in Awad (1963), p. 132. For a statement of the succession, see Choubert, Joly, Gigout, Marçais, Margat & Raynal (1956).   [5] Gigout (1957), pp. 27–38 and fig. 14 (35).
[6] Gigout (1960), p. 80.   [7] *Ibid.* p. 79.   [8] Beaudet & Maurer (1960), p. 45.

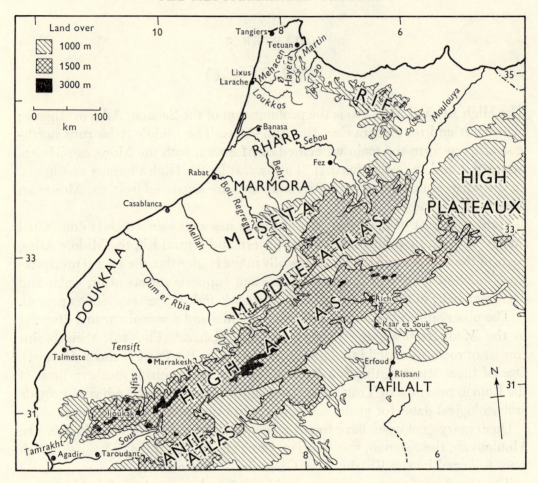

Fig. 30 Morocco: location map.

of the Last Glaciation. In some accounts the Rharbian is regarded as contemporaneous with the Flandrian (postglacial) transgression, on the grounds that it contains Neolithic artifacts and is graded to a fossil beach about 2 m above present sea-level;[1] in others it is placed after the Flandrian transgression.[2]

Two of the Moroccan exposures which have been cited as examples of a Flandrian raised beach were visited in the course of the present investigation. The situation at the mouth of Wadi Mellah was obscured by drifting sand, and in Wadi Lao the only feature which could reasonably be attributed to a recent high sea-level—a beach-rock formation—was *overlain* by Rharbian deposits.

---

[1] Beaudet & Maurer (1961), pp. 21–5; Beaudet, Destombes, Jeannette & Maurer (1960), pp. 10–11, 17–19. The Mellahian is the Moroccan equivalent of the Flandrian (Biberson, 1961, pp. 380–1; Gigout, 1957, pp. 7–12).

[2] Choubert (1962), p. 141, table I and *passim*. In table IV it is given a historical age; not so in table V.

As for the archaeological evidence, Biberson has pointed out that 'atypical' sherds found in the Rharbian have hitherto been regarded as Neolithic only because it was not thought possible that the deposits harbouring them could be of historical age.[1]

In fact, it has been known for some time that the Roman town of Banasa was buried by the Rharbian deposits of the Sebou (Pl. 27),[2] and charcoal from the *basse terrasse* of the Bou Regreg has given a radiocarbon date of 800 ± 200 years.[3] The evidence presented here gives further support to the contention that the Rharbian phase of aggradation is of historical age.

The Rharb plain is a suitable starting-point for this account. On the west it is separated from the sea by a line of dunes. On the north, northeast and east it is bounded by low hills, and on the south by the Marmora plateau. Four-fifths of the plain lies at an elevation of less than 20 m; its surface is broken by depressions (*merjas*) and by levee-like features along the Sebou and Beht rivers, whose banks can be over 10 m high. The smaller streams have ill-defined courses.

Since the Miocene, the Rharb has been filled by clayey sands to a maximum depth of over 250 m.[4] The formations exposed at the surface include redeposited Pliocene or Villafranchian material from the Marmora, dunes, marsh deposits in the *merjas*, and Soltanian and Rharbian alluvia. The Soltanian beds, following the usual pattern, tend to be red. The Rharbian has been divided by Pujos on the basis of colour into a black, lower (*ancien*) Rharbian of Neolithic age, and a grey, upper (*récent*) Rharbian, 'sub-actuel et actuel' in age.[5] The black soils, further subdivided according to the intensity of their blackness, are locally known as *tirs*; the grey soils as *dess*. Pedologic mapping reveals that these different soil types form bands parallel to the streams, and repeat the succession exposed in their banks. The younger and paler the deposit, the lower the clay content; this progressive coarsening of the alluvium carried by the Moroccan streams is further illustrated by the sandy nature of the modern flood-deposits (*mtill*). The factor of drainage, considered by Pujos,[6] is also relevant to the question of colour changes, as shown by the black soils which have developed in the *merjas*; stream downcutting, by improving drainage, may have led to conditions increasingly less conducive to *tirsification*.[7]

Roman sherds, as well as human bones, occur at a depth of 5 m in the banks of the Sebou at Moulay Ali Chrif, in a section previously described as exhibiting several superimposed buried soils dating from the lower Rharbian.[8] At Banasa, the banks are 9 m high (Pl. 28); recent excavations have discovered sherds of

[1] Biberson (1961), p. 196. [2] Gigout (1957), pp. 34–5; Choubert (1962), p. 171.
[3] Gigout (1959*a*), p. 2803; (1960), p. 138. The maximum reported height of this terrace is 8 m (Dresch and others, 1952, p. 155). [4] Ambroggi and others (1952), p. 153.
[5] Pujos (1958–9). [6] *Ibid.* p. 26. [7] *Ibid.* p. 20. [8] *Ibid.* p. 34.

Punic type (seventh to fifth century B.C.) at the base of the terrace, and Roman ruins are exposed 6 m higher, under 1·5 m of somewhat coarser alluvium.[1] Earlier accounts stated that the drains of the ancient town lie 3 m below the present river bottom,[2] and that the alluvium over the ruins is 3 m thick.[3] Deposition by floods such as those of 1951 and 1962 continues to modify the morphology of the plain; but the burial of Banasa by Rharbian alluvium cannot be disputed.

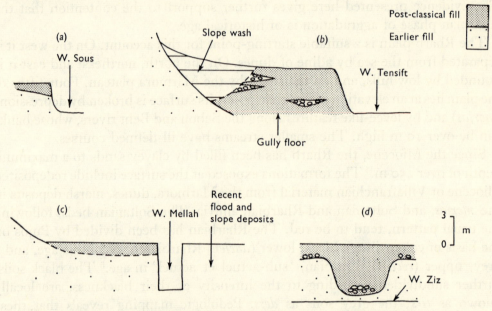

Fig. 31 Cross-sections: (a) Wadi Sous, west of Taroudant; (b) Wadi Tensif, near the coast road; (c) Wadi Mellah above the waterfall; (d) Wadi Ziz at Erfoud.

A Rharbian low terrace of grey alluvium has been reported from many other valleys, in the Rif, the Moroccan Meseta[4] (e.g. Wadi Mellah, Fig. 31c), Eastern Morocco,[5] the Doukkala,[6] and the Atlantic littoral.[7] It is also present in other parts of the country, and often contains Roman pottery.

An imposing example is the plain west of Tetuan which Wadi Martin, near its junction with the Hayera, has trenched to a depth of 5 m. Gullies near its margin show that here the deposit overlies scree from the slopes. The Mehacen near Larache has a similar fill: part of the ruins of ancient Lixus are buried by it.

Where it is crossed by the coast road, Wadi Tensif displays a lower terrace 5 m high (Pl. 29) whose well-defined rear edge and scored upper surface indicate

[1] Le Coz (1960); cf. Wilbert (1961), p. 21, who disagrees over the section at Souk el Tleta.
[2] Ambroggi and others (1952), p. 155 n. 1.   [3] See also Gigout (1957), p. 35.
[4] Beaudet & Maurer (1960).   [5] Raynal (1961), pp. 502, 517, 523, 528, 531, 556, 567.
[6] Choubert (1955), p. 35.   [7] Gigout (1957), pp. 28–31.

that it is occasionally flooded. It consists of fine-grained, well-bedded grey and pink-brown alluvium containing a few gravel lenses (Fig. 31 b). At one point, where the channel is 100 m across, the terrace remnant is over 300 m wide and contains sherds of historical age.[1] The deposit is also represented in tributaries of this stream, as in a small southern affluent 3 km south of Talmeste where the terrace is 3 m high. In the Tamrakht, 12 km north of Agadir (Pl. 30), the fill is 4 m thick, and contains sherds resembling those from Wadi Tensift. The Wadi Mellah fill has yielded charcoal dated by radiocarbon to 490±90 years ago.[2]

In Wadi Sous immediately to the west of Taroudant the low terrace may be seen on the right bank: 3 m of buff, indurated silt with its complement of sherds (Fig. 31 a). Further upstream, east of Taroudant, the banks of various tributaries of Wadi Sous consist of consolidated reddish silt with calcareous concretions, overlain by up to 4 m of incoherent well-bedded grey sand, silt and fine gravel. This material thins out laterally away from the stream, and fills gullies which are less steep-sided than those of today. No sherds could be found to confirm its identity with the Rharbian phase.

A 5 m terrace in Wadi Nfiss, 1 km south of Ijoukak (on the northern slopes of the Atlas), consists of medium and coarse rounded gravel overlain by red silty sand. A similar feature in Wadi Ziz, south of the Atlas watershed, is 6 m high 24 km south of Ksar es Souk, and 4 m high east of Rich, where it contains sherds of indistinct type.

Further downstream, in the oasis of Tafilalt, Wadi Ziz has been diverted for irrigation at various times, notably in the eighth–eleventh centuries (when the kingdom of Sigilmasa was most prosperous) and in the seventeenth and eighteenth centuries. Some of the dams employed for this purpose, for example that on the Irara dating from the seventeenth century, have a stepped construction reminiscent of the Roman dams on Wadi Megenin in Tripolitania.[3] According to Margat, alluvial deposition during the Rharbian produced terraces which are only 1–2 m high, whereas 5–8 m of silt were deposited in the palm groves as a consequence of flood-irrigation.[4]

In some reaches the banks of Wadi Ziz expose sections resembling that noted in Wadi Sous: a grey basal calcareous alluvium (here veined with iron and limonite) overlain unconformably by unconsolidated, cross-bedded, fine pink sand and silt (Fig. 31 d) (Pl. 32). The younger deposit may also be seen close to the ruins of Sigilmasa, near Rissani, where it has been gullied to a depth of 3 m (Pl. 31); here it contains numerous sherds—presumably derived from the ancient

[1] According to M. Souville and Lady Olwen Brogan; this is probably the 3–5 m terrace described by Dresch (1941), p. 480, and the Rharbian terrace described by Beaudet, Jeannette & Mazéas (1964), p. 48, and attributed by them tentatively to a higher sea-level.

[2] Lab no. I-2693 (May 1967).   [3] Margat (1962), p. 263, photo 22.   [4] Ibid. p. 59.

site—including some that cannot antedate the eleventh or twelfth century.[1] Both these lie outside the area that was repeatedly subjected to flood-irrigation. If these deposits are accepted as being not *limons de palmeraie* but the products of wadi aggradation, they show that the Rharbian of southern Morocco,[2] like that of northern Tripolitania, was being laid down during the Middle Ages.

[1] Information kindly supplied by M. Souville.
[2] For an account of Pleistocene valley fills in southeast Morocco, see Joly (1962). The Rharbian is discussed on pp. 262–8.

CHAPTER 6

SPAIN

Gigout has already remarked on the resemblance between the Quaternary deposits of the Moroccan and Spanish coasts, and identified deposits analogous to the Rharbian of Morocco on the eastern Spanish littoral, the recent alluvia of the principal rivers, the Ebro delta, part of the coastal plains, and small terraces in the lesser valleys.[1] Similar grey alluvial terraces, 2–3 m high, have been reported in the Llobregat and Besós valleys near Barcelona.[2] There are also many references in the literature to the presence in the major river basins of three or four Quaternary terraces,[3] the lowest of which will be considered below. Finally, we have two well-attested instances of historical deposition: in the Guadalentín Valley, where Arab irrigation works lie under 8 m of alluvium,[4] and at the mouth of the Guadalquivir, where the *lacus ligustinus* of the Romans has silted up.[5]

The Meseta, a great tableland which forms the core of Iberia, is rimmed by the Iberic Mountains, the Cantabrian Mountains and the Sierra Morena. Between the Iberic Mountains and the Pyrenees lies the Ebro trough, and between the Sierra Morena and the Andalusian Mountains the Guadalquivir valley.[6]

A threefold lithological subdivision has been proposed for Spain:[7] the argillaceous terrain of the Castilles and the Ebro and Guadalquivir lowlands; a zone marginal to the Meseta and including the peripheral mountain chains, where Mesozoic limestones produce tablelands separated by plains, bounded by scarps, and scored by gorges; and a western area of ancient siliceous rocks—granites, slates, schists and quartzites—eroded into rolling uplands and landscapes of low relief.

[1] Gigout (1959*b*).
[2] Solé (1962), p. 337. Marcet-Riba (1956), p. 636, has described 3–5 m terraces of grey silt and black soil in northeast Spain which he attributes to the Flandrian transgression. See also Ribeira-Faig (1950), p. 83.
[3] Hernández-Pacheco (1928); Solé and others (1952), pp. 146–7. The available descriptions, though sometimes painstakingly detailed (e.g. Nossin, 1959), are poor in relative or absolute dates and place undue emphasis on terrace height.
[4] Solé and others (1954), p. 92.
[5] Hernández-Pacheco (1932), p. 34; Solé and others (1952), p. 458 and fig. 186; Schulten (1955), pp. 332–3.
[6] Birot & Dresch (1953), I, 141–270; Solé and others (1952); Admiralty (1941).
[7] Solé and others (1954).

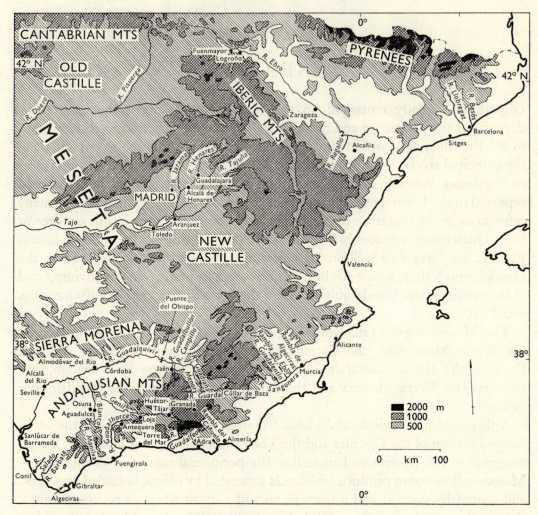

Fig. 32. Spain: location map.

The size and compactness of the peninsula and the presence of the coastal ranges combine to exclude maritime influences from the climate. Temperature extremes and widespread aridity result.

The uplands and coasts in the north and northwest receive over 800 mm of annual precipitation; the southeast is a sub-desert with an unreliable rainfall which may drop to less than 50 mm per annum.[1] The vegetation varies accordingly from deciduous forest to steppe, but large areas have been made bare because of the need for fuel, the appetite of herds and the ravages of war.[2]

[1] UNESCO-FAO (1963), pp. 27–8; Solé and others (1954), pp. 9–79.
[2] Solé and others (1954), pp. 145–271, esp. pp. 260–71.

66

Most of the Meseta drains away from the Mediterranean, the main watershed being the Iberic Mountains. Eastward drainage is limited to the narrow coastal strips and to the Ebro, which, abundantly supplied by the Pyrenees, enters the Mediterranean through a gorge in the coastal mountains. The river regimes predictably display great fluctuations in flow. In the drier areas it is common for the streams to function only during part of the year, usually in late winter and spring. Complications are introduced by the addition of snowmelt waters and, in the case of the larger basins, by the confluence of tributaries originating in different climatic zones.[1] The rivers shown on Fig. 32 range widely in size and in type of regime. Despite this, they display a striking consistency in their recent evolution.

Of the four alluvial terraces in the Guadalquivir drainage basin,[2] the lowest, 5–12 m high, contains Roman sherds. It is found in all parts of the catchment, and is usually composed of brown, incoherent fine sand and silt with gravel horizons, in contrast with the older terraces, which tend to be redder and often well cemented. The examples that follow show that the dimensions of the terrace bear little direct relationship to those of the reach in question.

The thickness of the fill exposed in the upper Guardal, near Cúllar de Baza (east of Jaén) is 8 m; in the Campillo, 32 km south of Jaén, it is 10 m; in a narrow left-bank tributary a short distance downstream of Córdoba, 5 m, and in another left-bank tributary south of Almodóvar del Río, where it is crossed by the road to Seville, 3 m. Here the terrace is unusually well-preserved, being over 200 m wide. The Genil, a major tributary of the Guadalquivir, displays a fragmentary lower terrace over 12 m high and up to 100 m wide on the right bank 3 km east of Loja. This deposit contains fragments of charcoal and what appears to be a Roman oven, exposed by recent digging. At Huétor-Tájar the terrace is only 6 m high but appears to underlie the entire plain, here over 1 km wide. The same applies to the Blanco valley at Aguadulce, where the fill is 6–10 m thick. In all these reaches the deposit yields Roman pottery. The soil of the *vegas* of Granada appears to have been derived from the same formation; its composition supports this inference, but no section deeper than 3 m is available, and intense cultivation makes it difficult to ascertain whether any artifacts it may contain are *in situ*.

The terrace also occurs within the main channel of the Guadalquivir, although it is often masked by recent flood deposits. Near Seville these form a bench about 5 m high within niches cut into the lower terrace; they are sandier, emphatically grey, and unconsolidated (Fig. 33c). Above Seville the terrace is 6–7 m high, but survives only as small remnants because it is more easily eroded

[1] Birot & Dresch (1953), fig. 22 (pp. 206–7); Hernández-Pacheco (1932), p. 26; Solé and others (1954), pp. 86–142. [2] Higueras (1961), pp. 32–3.

than the older fills. South of Alcalá del Rio (Fig. 33*d*) it forms well-defined terraces 8 m high (Pl. 33). Near the base of the deposit, a short distance downstream of the combined bridge-dam at Alcalá, protrude two walls 5 m apart; they are built of well-cut limestone blocks and probably date from Roman times. The rear edge of the terrace is indefinite, as it thins out over the older deposits that make up the rest of the plain, but it can be recognized about 10 km north of

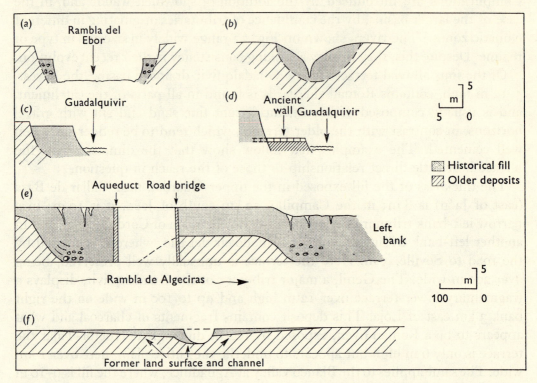

Fig. 33. Cross-sections: (*a*) Rambla del Ebor; (*b*) gully cut into older fill in Tagus near Toledo; (*c*) Guadalquivir above Seville; (*d*) Guadalquivir at Alcalá. Rambla de Algeciras: (*e*) left bank; (*f*) schematic cross-section of extent of fill.

Seville and 500 m east of the road from Alcalá to Seville (where quarrying of the older consolidated material has exposed the junction) and also across the river just south of a side road to Torre de la Reina. The fill thus appears to be at least 1 km in width at this point.

Further downstream the terrace broadens into a plain lying within the former estuary, and slopes down to meet the sea. A similar situation characterizes the mouths of smaller valleys on this coast, such as the Barbate and Salado.

The Tagus (Tajo) also underwent a phase of aggradation in historical times. One of its feeders, the Henares, flows within banks from 2 to over 4 m high cut into material whose lithology resembles that of the Guadalquivir terrace. Eight kilometres east of Alcalá de Henares, where it is crossed by the road to Santorcaz, the deposit is $\frac{1}{4}$ km wide; an older terrace with sherds misleadingly ploughed into it stands at 10 m. The lower terrace is also well defined southwest of Guadalajara. The Jarama river south of Madrid is incised by over 3 m into alluvium; in the Tajuna the terrace is lower still, and the reservations expressed with reference to the *vegas* of Granada apply to it.

In the Tagus immediately north of Aranjuez the low terrace is 2–4 m high and in some reaches over $\frac{1}{2}$ km wide. Further downstream, a few kilometres east of Toledo, two older terraces are well developed, one about 50 m high and composed of rounded gravel and reddish sand, the other 8 m high and composed of well-bedded, compact yellow and buff silt with fine gravel and coarse sand. Gullies eroded into the latter have been filled to a depth of 5 m by loose grey alluvium containing unidentifiable sherds (Fig. 33b). Finally, immediately upstream of the Alcántara bridge at Toledo, there is a well-defined 4 m terrace of brown alluvium (Pl. 34) which contains sherds, some of which are of Arab manufacture. The surface of this terrace forms the plain on the left bank of the river.

With the obvious exception of the Ebro basin, the valleys of the Mediterranean slopes tend to be too steep and narrow for the survival of unconsolidated alluvial terraces. The Guadalhorce, the longest of the streams that drain the southern slopes of the Andalusian mountains, has a 6 m terrace north of Antequera where it is crossed by the road to Córdoba. It consists of basal gravel overlain by sandy silt, and contains Roman pottery.

More often the deposit is well developed only at the mouths of the streams, where, as in the west, it forms either a flat deltaic plain or an alluvial fan at the foot of the coastal range. Good examples have formed at the mouths of the Guadalhorce and the Guadalfeo; the fertile *vegas* at Valencia and at other points on the Mediterranean coast of Spain owe much of their alluvium to this formation. The fans usually nestle within older deposits which, in the Manilva and in other valleys between Gibraltar and Málaga, resemble the older fans of the North African littoral in being composed of red earth and limestone gravel; in the more arid country between Adra and Murcia they are strongly cemented with calcium carbonate and sometimes coated with a calcareous crust.[1] It should be added that occasionally (as in the Rambla del Cañuelo, 19 km west of Almería) the alluvial fans have inherited their whitish-grey appearance from the marly country rock.

[1] Solé (1962), p. 336. According to Houston (1964), p. 4, deltas began to form along the coast between Málaga and Almería during the fifteenth and sixteenth centuries.

Some of the 'fans within fans' do not reach the sea, but merely slope down towards a major valley. Two instances will illustrate this: the Rambla del Ebor and the Rambla de Algeciras, both tributaries of the Sangonera River.

Forty-six kilometres southwest of Murcia, a gravel fill within the Rambla del Ebor is being exploited commercially. Its maximum exposed thickness is 5 m (Fig. 33 a). In years of heavy rain some of the excavated cavities are refilled by floodwaters; this accounts for a fragment of modern china found at a depth of 2 m within the deposit, which is otherwise rich in Roman sherds. Downstream of the Granada–Murcia road this material forms a 2 m terrace. A plausible interpretation is that the stream had cut down to a level consonant with its flood characteristics, and that, when excavation disturbed this condition, it was restored by aggradation during floods. But it is perhaps ingenuous to assume such efficiency in a stream that flows intermittently.[1]

About 22 km southwest of Murcia and 1 km southwest of Librilla, the Rambla de Algeciras has cut a ravine 12 m deep into reddish indurated silts to reveal in section older channels filled by ashy-grey, well-bedded silts, sands and gravels (Fig. 33 e). This fill, though locally well cemented, is generally unconsolidated. It contains Roman sherds at all levels, and has also yielded a basalt quern from its base. The distinctive colour of the historical fill can be observed in the soil as far as 2 km to the west of the Rambla, where it gives way to the prevailing redness of the piedmont slopes; in other words, once the channel had been filled, the alluvium 'overflowed' on to the surface which the channel had trenched (Fig. 33 f).

In the middle Ebro the terrace has survived principally within concave bends. Ten kilometres west of Logroño and immediately to the west of Fuenmayor, it forms an extensive lunate 5 m thick consisting of the familiar sandy silt with gravel beds; this has yielded abundant Roman pottery and one glazed (possibly medieval) sherd. Further downstream the terrace is more difficult to identify although, as in the Guadalquivir, it is better preserved in narrow tributaries; in the Rio Regallo, a ravine crossed by the road from Zaragoza 14 km west of Alcañiz, it is 5 m thick. Other valleys crossed by this road display the fill as yet uneroded.

The same material makes up much of the Ebro delta, and has given rise to broad terraces 5 m in height in the Llobregat valley between Sitges and Barcelona. Its identity with the formations described by Gigout and Solé cannot be doubted.

Attempts to date the end of deposition by reference to bridges of different

[1] Cf. Leopold, Wolman & Miller (1964), p. 238. Bennett (1960), pp. 59–60, describes the filling of *ramblas* by the products of contemporary erosion and the intentional diversion of stream debris into land that requires levelling.

ages were thwarted by their being either built on bedrock—as at Toledo—or sited in reaches where the terrace was absent—as with the Puente del Obispo on the Guadalquivir. But the behaviour of some of the *ramblas*, still engaged in fitful aggradation, shows that the Spanish streams do not act in strict unison: a date for the beginning or end of a particular phase in any one river would not necessarily apply to another. At present we cannot advance beyond the fact of widespread historical alluviation, locally extending into the Arab period.

CHAPTER 7

ITALY

A problem which was bound to arouse early speculation in Italy is the decay of areas whose prosperity was once proverbial, and whose ancient cities seem too grandiose for their present settings. Paestum was known to Martial for its violets and to Ovid and Virgil for its roses; Metapontum sent a crown of golden ears of corn to Delphi;[1] today they lie in Italy's Poor South. But it is not always clear how much needs to be explained: the old descriptions may well have been distorted by lyricism; and the finest ruins are temples which needed no humus.

Some changes are clear-cut and familiar. Rivers that were navigable in Classical times, and in some instances as late as the sixteenth century, have silted up.[2] The course of lowland streams has altered and continues to do so.[3] Former seaports—notably Ostia[4]—now lie inland as a result of deposition at their mouths. Indeed, many Italian deltas have formed almost entirely in historical times,[5] although at varying rates: the Tiber delta, for example, grew faster during the Middle Ages than during Roman times,[6] and the expansion of the Po delta accelerated sharply during the thirteenth century.[7]

Archaeological dating has been applied to river deposits inland, most successfully in southern Etruria, north of Rome and between the Tiber and the sea. Here Ward Perkins had found early Iron Age and Roman remains buried by the alluvium into which the streams have cut trenches 3–8 m deep.[8] From a study of various sites and buried objects, Judson concluded that, although some of this alluvium was laid down between A.D. 50 and 209, deposition took place chiefly between late Imperial and early medieval times, and this has been confirmed by two radiocarbon dates. A map of 1534 showed that stream incision had been accomplished by that date. Judson found a similar deposit forming a terrace 4–5 m high, and containing ancient and medieval sherds, in the Gornalunga valley of east-central Sicily (see Fig. 35 a).[9]

The observations outlined below were made in other parts of ancient Etruria

---

[1] D'Arrigo (1956), p. 659.   [2] *Ibid.* pp. 6–8, 10–11.   [3] Ortolani & Alfieri (1947).

[4] Meiggs (1960), pp. 51–2, 115.   [5] Marinelli (1926); Piccardi (1956).

[6] Bradford (1957), p. 246, although Ward Perkins (1962, p. 397) states that by the beginning of the Christian era the growth of the Tiber delta had already rendered Ostia virtually unusable and forced its citizens to raise the level of the streets and houses twice within two centuries.

[7] Marinelli (1926), p. 24.   [8] Ward Perkins (1962), pp. 396–7.

[9] Judson (1963a, 1963b). Valchetta valley and the La Crescenza valley: $1,140 \pm 160$ years B.P. (I-881) and $1,400 \pm 100$ years B.P. (I-882) (personal communication by Dr Judson).

(within present-day Latium and Tuscany) and in Campania (Fig. 34). The former is a part of the pre-Apennines which has been broken up into small physiographic components by faulting and volcanic activity; it is drained principally by the Tiber and the Arno. Campania includes offshoots of the Apennines among which nestle small alluvial plains and volcanoes, some of them still active.[1]

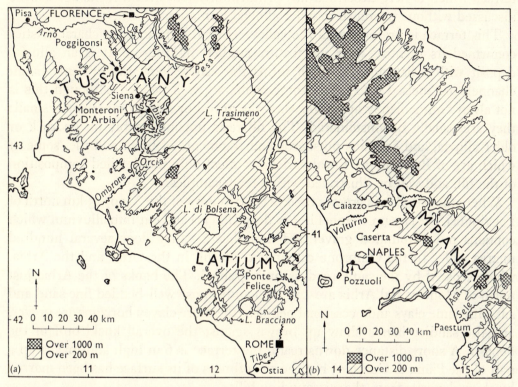

Fig. 34. Central Italy: location maps, (a) Tuscany and Latium, (b) Campania.

In this part of central Italy the annual rainfall ranges from 500 to 3,000 mm,[2] largely according to elevation. The river regimes[3] are characterized by low water in summer and by spring and autumn floods, although large areas of limestone in Campania and in the southern half of the Tiber basin reduce the range of variations in the discharge. What vegetation survives includes open scrub, macchia, and patches of woodland.

The Tuscan uplands consist of Permian sandstones, some older crystalline rocks, and Mesozoic limestones. Large areas are occupied by plateaux composed

[1] Birot & Dresch (1953), I, 273–310; Admiralty (1944), I, 266–300.
[2] UNESCO-FAO (1963), pp. 29–30.　　　　[3] Toniolo (1950), pp. 445–50.

73

of tuffs and other volcanic rocks, and by Pliocene clays, sands, marls and sand-stones. In Campania, limestones (chiefly Cretaceous) form the mountains of the north, and lavas and volcanic tuffs make up the remaining hills. There are also extensive stretches of Pleistocene alluvium, particularly on the coast.

No convincing scheme for the stream terraces of these areas or for their correlation with littoral deposits has hitherto been formulated.[1] But, as the terrace which is here described has plentiful artifacts within it, its age can be discussed without reference to older alluvial formations.

This terrace is present in all the valleys visited. Certain of its characteristics confirmed its identity with the feature studied by Judson. It is an alluvial deposit with a flat surface which forms the valley floor; the present stream channels are incised into it. Its components are well bedded, although this is not always immediately apparent when the gravel or sand component is small; they are usually unconsolidated. The fill rests unconformably on bedrock or older alluvia, and contains potsherds and fragments of brick and tile, some of which are of Roman age. Local variations affect only the detailed composition of the fill, and will be illustrated with a few examples.

Where the Via Cassia crosses the Pesa (a tributary of the Arno) 15 km north of Poggibonsi, the stream channel is 4 m deep (Pl. 35) and cut into alluvium which contains much rounded gravel and underlies a valley floor several hundred metres wide. In the Ombrone catchment, the fill in the Orcia and the Arbia, where crossed by the same road, is finer grained. The banks of the Arbia just north of Monteroni d'Arbia are 4 m high and expose well-bedded fine sand and silt with some clays and occasional pebbles; the more clayey horizons are greyer, and the sandier bands show up brown against the overall khaki buff of the deposit. A short distance downstream, the terrace is 6 m high and makes up a part of the Piana di Curiano; but the smoothness of its surface has been marred by slope deposits from the surrounding hills.

In the Tiber valley between Ponte Felice and Rome,[2] the river banks are 4–6 m high above water-level and offer few good sections. The material making up the plain is very similar to that of the Arno and Ombrone terraces. Ponte Felice itself, rebuilt in 1949, was begun at the end of the sixteenth century under Sixtus V and finished under Clement VIII. Its foundations suggest that the stream had by that time cut its present channel.

For parts of its course the Volturno flows below the level of a broad plain. A good section is exposed on the left bank downstream of the bridge that carries the road from Caserta to Caiazzo; here 8 m of grey clay and sand, brown and plastic when wet, contain a few thin lenses of angular limestone gravel.

[1] Selli (1962), p. 408.   [2] For a detailed survey of this reach, see Tevere (1954).

Thirteen kilometres south of Salerno, the Torrente Asa is crossed by the Paestum road. It is cut into a flat-topped formation which makes up most of the Sele plain. Within this channel there is a terrace 5 m high which, though fragmentary, can be recognized by its content of potsherds and its characteristic

(a)

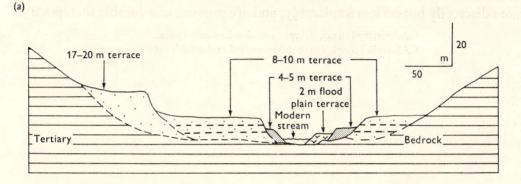

(b)

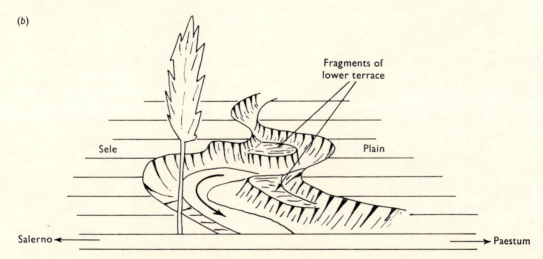

Fig. 35. (a) Cross-section of Gornalunga valley, east-central Sicily (after Judson, 1963b, fig. 3); (b) terrace remnants in Sele valley above coast road.

silty sand with bands of fine gravel (Fig. 35b). The Sele itself has a similar terrace some tens of metres wide.

Other cases of post-Classical aggradation can be inferred from contemporary accounts. Thus it appears that in the eleventh century the mountain tributaries of the Chiana, another tributary of the Arno, began to silt up the main river[1] and turned the vale into a swamp.[2] This may also explain the fact that 'like so

[1] Admiralty (1944), I, 284.　　　[2] Fossombroni (1823); Semple (1931), 545.

75

much of the west coast of Italy, the plain of Pisa became increasingly marshy during the Middle Ages'.[1]

The present day presents a picture of widespread and violent erosion (Pl. 36),[2] particularly in areas of Pliocene bedrock: hillsides are gullied and settlements undermined. The deltas continue to grow. The historical alluvia are attacked more discreetly but no less implacably, and are proving less durable than poetry.

[1] Admiralty (1944), p. 271; see also Losacco (1962).
[2] Almagià (1907), (1910); Morandini and others (1962).

CHAPTER 8

GREECE

In his *Principles of Geology*,[1] Lyell quotes M. Boblaye to the effect that in the Morea

the formation termed céramique, consisting of pottery, tiles and bricks, intermixed with various works of art, enters so largely into the alluvium and vegetable soil upon the plains of Greece, and into hard and crystalline breccias which have been formed at the foot of declivities, that it constitutes an important stratum, which might, even in the absence of zoological characters, serve to mark part of the human epoch in a most indestructible manner.

The statement makes it admirably clear that the fate of Olympia—one of the works of art in Greece thus buried—is but an instance of a widespread phenomenon. This chapter will discuss the problem with reference to some of the valleys of central, southern and northwestern Greece (Fig. 36).[2]

In the Peloponnese, a mass of rugged highlands is fringed on the west and north by a belt of foothills and by a narrow coastal plain; over half the area rises above 500 m, and there is little flat land. Central Greece is typified by broad alluvial plains separated by mountain blocks. Epirus consists of a series of folded ranges whose ruggedness belies the fact that they rarely exceed a height of 2,000 m; they are aligned roughly north–south and are trenched by deep gorges. Numerous bays and gulfs allow the influence of the Mediterranean Sea to penetrate deeply into Greece,[3] but this is countered by the mountainous nature of much of the country; the interior of Epirus on occasion can experience winter temperatures as low as −12 °C. The mean annual precipitation varies from 400 mm in the east to over 1,200 mm in the Pindus, with violent fluctuations from year to year. The vegetation reflects the wide range of conditions available, so that, in addition to the usual range of Mediterranean associations, one encounters deciduous and coniferous forests in the highlands.

The limestones that dominate the geological maps of these areas are chiefly of Mesozoic and Miocene age.[4] Extensive zones are also occupied by Cretaceous and Tertiary *flysch*, igneous and metamorphic rocks, and Quaternary alluvium. The last includes extensive red beds which give rise to fans on the coast and high terraces inland.[5]

[1] Lyell (1872), II, 520.   [2] Admiralty (1945), III, and Philippson (1950–9), *passim*.
[3] Admiralty (1944), I, 78–105; UNESCO-FAO (1963), pp. 31–2.
[4] Admiralty (1945), III, figs. 13 and 29; Aubouin and others (1963); Paraskevaidis (1956).
[5] Higgs and Vita-Finzi (1966), pp. 2–8.

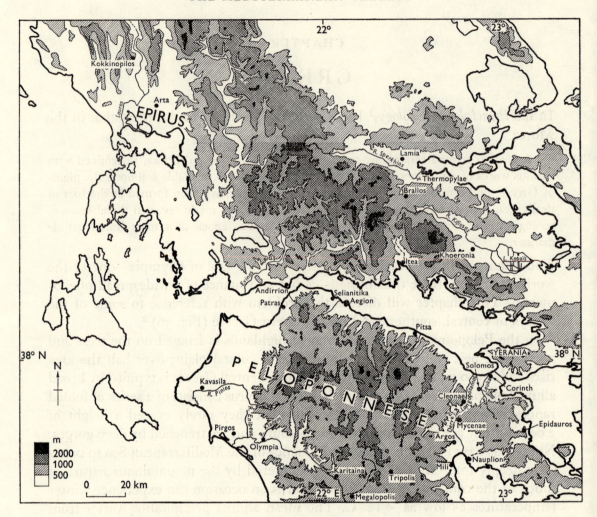

Fig. 36. Greece: location map.

The Alfios makes a good starting-point for a study of the final retouches made to the landscape by stream action. The course of this river, the largest in the peninsula, includes both sediment-filled plains and narrow cuttings through resistant rock ridges; it drains a great structural depression which is floored in part by Pliocene beds.[1] The Alfios is bordered by high terraces—well displayed at Megalopolis—and by alluvial fans. It opens out into the coastal plain at its confluence with the Kladeos. Here lie the ruins of Olympia, overlooked by marl hills clothed in maquis and pines.

Ellsworth Huntington was, perhaps, the first to realize that the alluvium under

[1] Admiralty (1945), III, 187–92.

which Olympia lay (Pl. 37) is part of a deposit that 'extends for miles up and down the Alpheios and its tributaries',[1] rather than the local feature described by the excavators. But he does not mention that a similar formation is to be found in other Greek rivers; his interest lay in Asia and that is where he sought his analogies.[2]

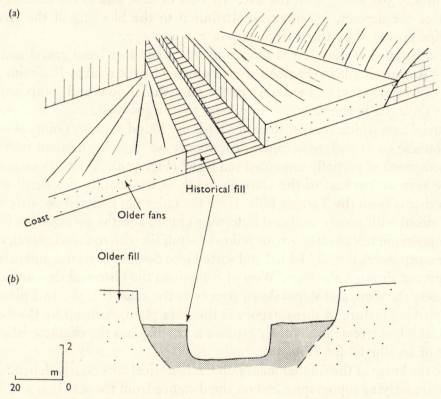

Fig. 37. (a) 'Nested' fans on Peloponnese coast; (b) younger fill in stream crossed by road to Tripolis 5 km southwest of Mili.

At Olympia, the Kladeos has cut down to the base of the deposit, which is 6 m thick and composed of fine sand and silt, with lenses and beds of rounded gravel. Many ancient structures are covered by the alluvium; some of them can be seen upstream of the main site. There is also pottery in profusion.

It is a luxury to date the alluvium with a city of beauty rather than with broken pots, rubble and utilitarian dams. But Olympia is also of value in that it provides a more accurate *post quem* date than usual. To begin with, one of the structures

[1] Huntington (1901), p. 662. Cf. Brooks (1926), p. 355, who states that 'unfortunately the hydrographical system of this river is so peculiar that it is doubtful whether any significance can be attached to this deposit of silt'. [2] Huntington (1901), pp. 665–7.

buried by streamlaid alluvium was a Byzantine fortress.[1] Prehistoric remains under the Greek occupation levels are also buried by rock debris and soil, but the evidence given in the excavation reports suggests that this was the work of slope-wash from the hill of Kronos,[2] and not the flooding postulated by Gardiner. Secondly, there was no alluvial deposition until after squatters had dropped coins of A.D. 565 and 575 on the site.[3] In view of this, and of the lithology and extent of the deposit, it cannot be attributed to the blocking of the river by landslips provoked by the earthquakes of 522 and 557.[4]

Local parallels include a 3 m terrace of sandy silt over basal gravel and containing Roman sherds in the small stream crossed by the road to Karitaina 5 km north of Megalopolis; and a terrace of the same dimensions and composition as that at Olympia in the Enipeus river, near the Pirgos road.

Alluvial fans which contain Roman sherds are found at many points along the Peloponnese coast and, as in Spain, commonly occupy channels cut into older fans composed of partially cemented red beds[5] (Fig. 37a). An excellent example can be seen 10 km east of the Corinth canal, at the mouth of a small stream which drains from the Yerania hills. Here the older fan material consists of red earth mixed with poorly rounded limestone gravel, and the younger fan (which has a maximum thickness of 6 m) of yellowish-buff silt with rounded gravel, which in some exposures is well bedded and sorted into distinct horizons, and in others is dispersed through the fines. West of Selianitika the historical deposit is 10 m thick near the road, and slopes down steeply to the coast (Pl. 38). In Epirus, the most striking feature in this category is the Arta plain, built up by the Louros and Arakhthos rivers: it fills their estuaries, yet displays the characteristic convexity of an alluvial fan (Fig. 38).

The thickness of the fill that makes up the historical fans clearly depends both on the underlying topography and on the distance from the sea. It is 5 m in the Pinios river, south of Kavasila, where it is crossed by the coast road, 2–3 m above the road bridge west of Aegion, and 2 m upstream of the road-crossing 5 km southwest of Mili, where the older fill is 4 m thick (Fig. 37b). The relationship between older and newer fans is equally diagrammatic east of Pitsa and about 5 km east of Patras.

The formation is displayed in a variety of other situations; its composition and extent vary in a manner that is by now familiar. Immediately south of Solomos, the Leuka is incised 6–8 m into the fill, here composed of well-cemented silt and sand, beds of clay, and coarse, iron-stained sand over a

---

[1] Gardiner (1925), p. 5.

[2] Dörpfeld (1935), II, Tafel 7, Profile of *Idaïsche Grotte und Heraklesaltar*, showing a steeply-dipping humus horizon. For a similar horizon under the Metroön, see Gardiner (1925), p. 12.

[3] Gardiner (1925), p. 5.   [4] *Ibid.*   [5] Mistardis (1950).

sub-rounded basal gravel. Red soil interstratified with gravel and sand pre-dominates in the $3\frac{1}{2}$ m section exposed by stream-trenching of the plain near ancient Cleonae in the upper Longopotamos. In the banks of the small stream crossed by the side road to Mycenae, the fill has a maximum thickness of 4 m

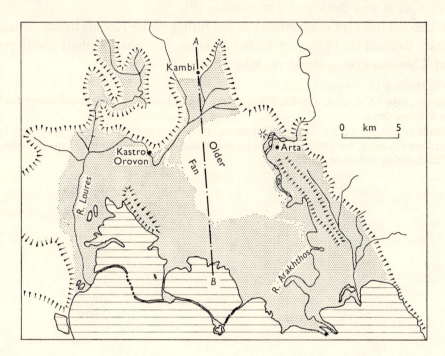

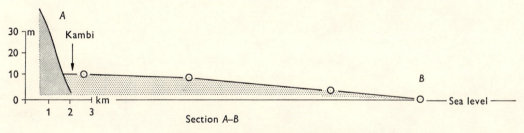

Fig. 38. The Arta plain of Epirus.

and is characterized by brown silt, fine sand, and sub-rounded gravel. In these three areas, and also north of Itea, aggradation in historical times has filled in gullies and channels cut into older alluvia and given the finishing touches to the fashioning of a plain. Similarly, 27 km south of Tripolis, gullies eroded into a red clay deposit within an intermontane basin have been filled with alluvium containing sherds to a maximum depth of 3 m; the gullies are now being re-excavated. In essentially the same situation at Kokkinopilos, near Agios

Georgios (Epirus), the fill contains fragments of brick from the *spiramina* of a Roman aqueduct which had been driven through the clays. It lies in channels cut below the land surface of Roman times.[1] In the valley followed by the road to Epidauros, the fill is $3\frac{1}{2}$ m thick; in a tributary of the Evinos, 15 km northwest of Andirrion, it is 5 m thick and 500 m wide (Pl. 39).

The deposit has also contributed to the filling of the Kopaïs basin, which was artificially drained in 1886, and to the creation of a coastal plain about 7·5 km wide at Thermopylae, a defile no longer.[3]

[1] Dakaris, Higgs & Hey (1964), p. 213.
[2] Philippson (1950–9), II, pt. i, 467–84, discusses the earlier history of the lake and states that it was dry in Minoan times.
[3] Béquignon (1937), pp. 43, 55. See also Philippson (1950–9), I, 240, and map in Guide Bleu (1962), p. 669; Cary (1949), p. 65. Other estuaries, including those of the Kokkitos and the Acheron, have been filled during and since Antiquity.

CHAPTER 9

JORDAN

[a]ggradation in the eastern Mediterranean has already been re-
[...] [work]ers. In Wadi Ghuzzeh, south of Gaza, Petrie noted 50 ft
[... of] clayey silt containing late Roman pottery;[1] in Israel, Guy found[2]
[that ...] of alluvium had been laid down in Wadi Musrara since Roman or
Byzantine times. In Syria, 'There was soil upon the northern hills where none
now exists, for the buildings now show unfinished foundation courses which
were not intended to be seen; the soil in depressions without outlets is deeper
than it formerly was';[3] and, according to Van Liere,[4] the Euphrates fashioned
its main bed and flood-plain after medieval times. Earlier events also recall the
Tripolitanian succession. According to Evenari and his collaborators, during the
Nabatean period the major Negev wadis were 'wide shallow depressions
meandering in alluvial plains' on which flood-spreading could be practised;
later, probably in Roman and Byzantine times, they cut deep gullies in which
diversion structures were built.[5] The area considered by this chapter lies in
Jordan, where inland drainage provides (as in the Tafilalt of Morocco) a geological sequence divorced from sea-level influences.

The streams under consideration flow into the great trench occupied by the
Jordan valley, the Dead Sea and the Wadi 'Araba (Fig. 39). To the west lie the
mountains of Judea, Samaria and Galilee, to the east the plateau of what used to
be called Transjordan, on the edge of Arabia. The Dead Sea lies at 392 m below
sea-level, and on either side of it the land rises to over 1,000 m. Climate and
vegetation are correspondingly diverse. The mean annual precipitation ranges
from less than 50 to over 900 mm, and supports desert, steppe, *maquis*, and
occasionally Mediterranean forest communities. Where there are no springs, the
streams are dry in summer and flow intermittently in winter.[6]

It is a land rich in human debris of all ages,[7] and this can be turned to the
advantage of Quaternary geology. The absence of Neolithic and Bronze Age
remains from the Jordan flood-plain, for example, was the basis for Picard's
estimate of its age.[8] But this account is more concerned with later times, when

[1] Petrie (1928), p. 16.   [2] Guy (1958), p. 86.
[3] Butler (1920) quoted by Huntington & Visher (1922), p. 69.
[4] Van Liere (1960–1), p. 48.   [5] Evenari and others (1961), pp. 991–2.
[6] Admiralty (1943), pp. 47–61; UNESCO-FAO (1963), p. 35.
[7] Harding (1960). See also Smith (1894), and Huntington (1911).
[8] Picard (1943), p. 158.

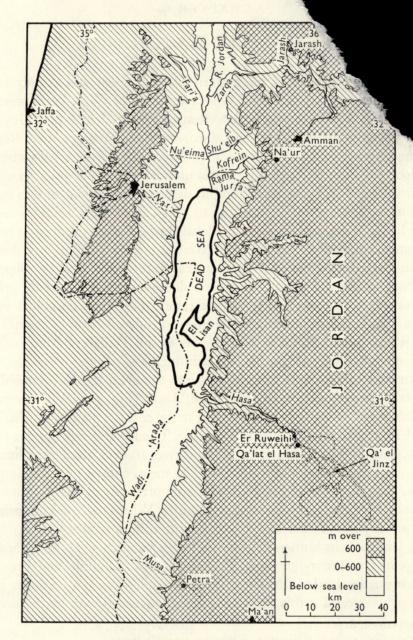

Fig. 39. Central Jordan: location map.

ᴅead, Moab and Edom came under the Nabateans,

ʼrocks of the African–Arabian shield form the Aqaba
ᴀᴇ south of the country.[1] On this basement were deposited

Post-Classical ᴀ
ᴘorted by otʰ
(14·4 m) of ᴀ
ᵗʰᵃᵗ 7 ᴍ

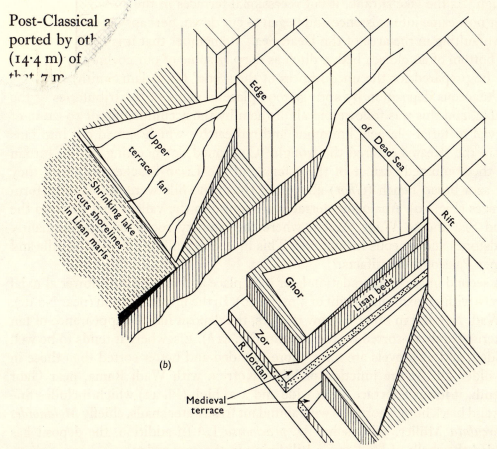

Fig. 40. Block-diagrams showing (a) development of Upper Terrace fans, and (b) *Ghor* and *Zor*.

sandstones dating from the Cambrian to the Lower Cretaceous, and then limestones, dolomites, chalks and marls until the Eocene, when folding preceded the
Miocene fracturing responsible for the Rift Valley. Later deposition was either
terrestrial or lacustrine. In the north, lavas were erupted from the Miocene
almost into historical times. Miocene and Pliocene limestones and marls laid
down in the Rift were affected by renewed tectonic movement; the accumulation
of the Pleistocene Lisan Series followed.

This comprises a lower stage with conglomerates and lacustrine beds, and,

[1] Picard (1943), p. 158, and Burdon (1959).

separated from it by faulting, an upper stage during which a vast lake extended from Tiberias to south of the Dead Sea. In it were laid down the Lisan marls, a varved sediment consisting of thin layers rich in gypsum alternating with more clayey-calcareous bands that passes into coarse gravels at the margins of the trough. As the lake shrank, it cut recessional terraces in the marls. The Jordan river now came into existence and began to cut down, perhaps helped by further downfaulting in the area of the Dead Sea. 'Remember that it is but a groove in the bottom of an old sea bed, a ditch as deep as some of our coalmines, and you will be prepared for the uncouthness of the scene' (G. Adam Smith).[1]

Tufaceous deposition by springs took place in some of the tributaries of the Jordan, and this was followed in all of them by the accumulation of 10–20 m of alluvial material—largely limestone and red earth—which spread out into fans where the streams entered the trough.[2] Continued downcutting by the Jordan left the combined surface of these fans and the Lisan beaches on which they rest as a broad bench (*Ghor*) above the river; the fills were trenched to form terraces (Fig. 40). Analogous terraces are found in the valleys that drain to the Dead Sea and to Wadi 'Araba, where the country rocks are predominantly sandstones and igneous formations. This first valley fill has yielded Middle and Upper Palaeolithic artifacts.[3]

A second phase of aggradation later took place and resulted in a lower alluvial terrace with a maximum height of 5 m (Pl. 40). In the upper Kofrein (near Na'ur), in Wadi Nar and in other narrow reaches, the deposit has the appearance of fan material barely re-sorted by the stream (Fig. 41 *b*). Elsewhere it tends to be well bedded, and its gravels are finer, more rounded and better sorted than those in the older fill. At the junction of Wadi Kofrein with Wadi Rama, near Gabr Effendi, it forms a terrace 30 m wide and 4 m high (Pl. 42) which includes fine silts and black humic horizons with abundant freshwater snails, chiefly *Melanoides tuberculata* Müller, with some *M. praemorsa* L.[4] In addition, the deposit has yielded the shells of land snails still living in the area today.

This fill contains Iron Age, Bronze Age, Roman and Byzantine sherds at all levels; in Wadi Musa, Nabatean types are also included. At Petra the terrace partly covers remains of Roman age (Pl. 41), and in Wadi Fari'a (west of the Jordan) a Roman dam. In Wadi Hasa, at Er Ruweihi, it contains both Roman and Arab sherds, and overlies rubble that includes fragments of polished marble (Fig. 41 *d*).

In part of Wadi Nu'eima the terrace occupies a narrow gorge cut into bedrock;

---

[1] Smith (1894), p. 85. [2] The *Oberterrasse* and *Blockschotter delta* of Picard (1938), p. 15.
[3] Vita-Finzi (1964).
[4] Sparks *in* Vita-Finzi (1964), pp. 32–3. Cf. the grey-black marly loam associated with the Meso-Neolithic by Picard (1932, quoted by Butzer 1958*a*, p. 114).

any earlier alluvia have been removed from it (Fig. 41 c). Usually, as in Wadis Er Ruabi (see Pl. 43) and Shu'eib, it lies in channels cut into the older fill (Fig. 41 a). In the Jordan valley it makes up part of the *Zor*, the rest of which (though often buried by recent flood deposits) is merely a bench cut into the Lisan marls. Picard's view of its age[1] is thus vindicated.

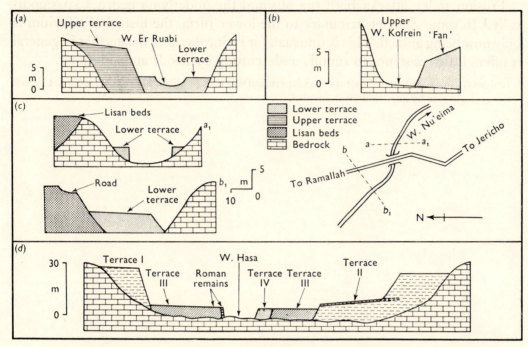

Fig. 41. Cross-sections: (a) Wadi Er Ruabi; (b) upper Wadi Kofrein; (c) Wadi Nu'eima; (d) Wadi Hasa near Qa'lat El Hasa.

In the upper Wadi Hasa, the sequence is more complicated (see Fig. 42 d). The uppermost terrace consists of highly calcareous silt and contains Middle Palaeolithic artifacts; Kebaran artifacts lie on its surface. The second terrace forms tongues of gravel about 2 m thick in embayments cut into the first, and yields pre-Kebaran Upper Palaeolithic artifacts. The third terrace underlies much of the valley floor and contains Kebaran remains; the present stream is entrenched below it. At Er Ruweihi, where a tributary of that name joins the main stream $2\frac{1}{2}$ km downstream of Qa'lat El Hasa, the fourth terrace (the equivalent of the lower terrace in other wadis) is about 3 m high and consists of fine sand, silt and gravel.

[1] Schattner (1962), p. 120, suggests that the Jordan flood plain is still being built up by meandering. If so, this is merely contributing to an existing feature. Cf. Ionides (1939), p. 219, who believed that the minor valley of the Jordan was a product of erosion and showed no obvious sign of deposition.

The width of the historical deposit is restricted by the channels it fills (Fig. 41 *b*), and amounts to a few metres except where the valley opens out at its junction with another stream. Where Wadi Jarash enters the River Zerqa, the terrace widens into a broad 'delta', and where Wadi Musa debouches into Wadi 'Araba it has formed an extensive alluvial fan.

Erosion today attacks both the fills and the underlying bedrock spasmodically.[1] In some channels tributary to the lower Jurfa, the historical alluvium is only now being gullied. This is unusual, for its incoherence means that in general it offers little resistance to runoff, undercutting by floods and slumping.

[1] Ionides (1939), p. 215, stated that spectacular erosion was rare and (*ibid*. p. 219) that it did not exceed the geologic rate by any significant amount.

PART II

PART II

CHAPTER 10

THE POSTGLACIAL EVOLUTION OF THE MEDITERRANEAN VALLEYS

The burden of Part I may be restated as follows. At some stage during historical times, many of the streams in the Mediterranean area, which had hitherto been engaged primarily in downcutting, began to build up their beds (Fig. 42). The effect of this alluvial aggradation was to steepen and smooth out the longitudinal stream profiles. The process is shown schematically in Fig. 43 a; an attempt has also been made to indicate that, in all but the smallest catchments, historical aggradation did not produce a single continuous alluvial surface but rather a stairway of such surfaces (analogous to the succession of soil terraces accumulated by the Roman soil dams of Tripolitania) which were separated by those breaks in the bed slope that were too abrupt to be masked by the alluvium.

Renewed downcutting, still in operation today, has since incised the channels into the alluvial fill, and is tending to flatten the longitudinal profiles. Their stepped character is being thereby restored, and the successive reaches are linked by rapids and waterfalls (Fig. 43 b).

It is this sequence of events—valley filling followed by downcutting—which has given the Mediterranean valleys their characteristic form: a well-defined channel cut into a broad, smooth valley floor.[1] The valley floor is the surface of the historical fill; it is reached only by exceptional floods and this generally only near the river mouths where the channel is at its shallowest. The true flood plain[2] (or *lit majeur*) is developed at the expense of the fill, and lies below its surface.

Geologists have burned their fingers often enough to reach for their fire extinguishers when they hear the word 'correlation' applied to events during the million years or more spanned by the Quaternary Era; they prefer terms like 'equivalence' to the commitment of 'simultaneity'.[3] One might conclude, *a fortiori*, that there has not been time in the last 2,000 years for the manifestation of geological changes widespread and profound enough to justify inclusion in the stratigraphic table. This chapter is devoted to placing the events that concern us in the wider context of geological history, and to an analysis of their magnitude and chronology.

[1] Birot & Dresch (1953), I, 22.
[2] Leopold and others (1964), pp. 317–28.
[3] Boulaine (1957), p. 442.

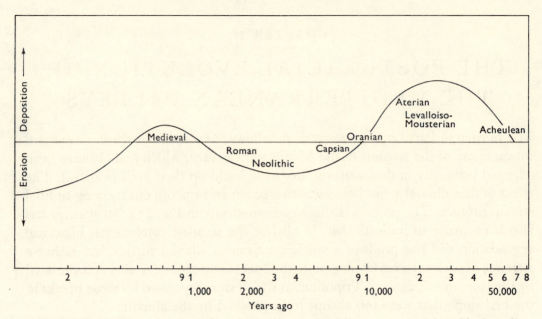

Fig. 42. Chronology of erosion and deposition in the Mediterranean area. A logarithmic scale has been used for the time base solely in order to accommodate the diagram on one page.

The older fill

The floor of the Mediterranean valleys is commonly bordered by well-preserved alluvial terraces which rest against the bedrock of the interfluves. These terraces represent an older phase of valley filling. Still earlier deposits are also present, but they are generally restricted to patches resting on benches cut in bedrock; doubtless they also lurk here and there under the historical alluvium. As we have seen, in some areas the older fill rests on tufa deposits precipitated by springs. In others, its lower horizons are cemented by calcium carbonate and this gives rise to a hardpan which extends laterally as a crust capping the local bedrock. The crusts occasionally grade into tufas.

Many workers have concluded that the older fill accumulated more or less concurrently throughout the Mediterranean basin.[1] According to Arambourg, it serves as 'un niveau repère absolument constant' in the coastal areas between Atlantic Morocco and Syria.[2] Butzer places the deposition of this 'heterogeneous class of colluvial silts and alluvial gravels' at the beginning of the Last Glaciation.[3]

The older fill is indeed of great lithological diversity, ranging from angular scree to clay. Yet certain characteristics which it displays in all the areas discussed

[1] See Butzer (1964), *passim*; Demangeot (1956), p. 41; Vaufrey (1955), p. 97; Balout (1955), p. 49.
[2] Arambourg (1951), p. 49. [3] Butzer (1963*b*), pp. 212–13.

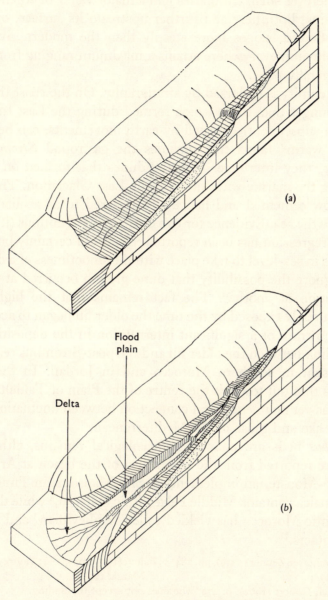

Fig. 43. (a) Morphology of younger fill at close of aggradation. (b) Trenching of younger fill accompanied by deltaic extension. (The older fill has been omitted for the sake of clarity.)

in this book justify its recognition as a single phase. To begin with it is dominated by material rich in red iron oxides. More significantly, it assumes the form of an alluvial fan wherever small tributaries join a major valley or when streams enter the coastal plains. Both here and further upstream its surface, over which the streams once flowed, slopes more steeply than the modern river beds. The thickness of alluvium everywhere attains a maximum ranging from 20 to 40 m; bedding is generally poor.

Topographic unity is endorsed by stratigraphy. On the coast the fans overlie beaches no younger than those which formed during the Last Interglacial and which, though subsequently warped by earth movements, can be identified by a distinctive 'warm' fauna that includes the gastropod *Strombus bubonius*.[1] What is more, they interfinger with the dunes that formed on the *Strombus* beaches during the marine withdrawal of the Last Glaciation. These regressive aeolianites (now cemented and hence also referred to as aeolian calcarenites) continue below the sea. Evidence for two or three interruptions (if not reversals) of the marine regression has been reported.[2] It would certainly be ingenuous to expect changes in sea-level to take place with the smoothness of a draughtsman's curve, or to ignore the possibility that dune growth occurred at one stage and stream deposition at another. The fact remains that the highest *Strombus* beaches were already exposed by the time the older fill began to accumulate, and that there is no trace of a significant interruption in the deposition of the fill. The intimate link between the older fill and the post-*Strombus* regressive sea is, of course, absent in southern Morocco and in Jordan. In the former, the Soltanian beds thin out towards the centre of the Plain of Tafilalt,[3] while in the latter there is as yet no unequivocal connection between fluctuations in the level of the Lisan Lake and those of the Mediterranean.

The *Strombus* beds are poor in archaeological remains, although Aterian implements are reported from the upper part of the beach at Arzew, Algeria,[4] and Levalloiso-Mousterian implements at Sidi Mansour, in Tunisia.[5] The 6 m beach of Cyrenaica contains Middle Palaeolithic material,[6] while the Tyrrhenian beach of Atlantic Morocco has yielded rolled 'Abbevillian' and slightly rolled Acheulean artifacts.[7]

---

[1] For general accounts see Zeuner (1959), pp. 284–5; Balout (1955), pp. 51–2; Vaufrey (1955), pp. 51–2.

[2] E.g. Hilly (1962), p. 359.   [3] Margat (1962), p. 64.

[4] Camps (1955); cf. Gobert (1962), p. 279, who does not accept the finding.

[5] Castany (1962), pp. 263, 279. Balout (1955), p. 123, asserts that the *Strombus* fauna is pre-Aterian. Vaufrey (1955), p. 98 n. 1, cites evidence to the effect that the continental deposits contemporaneous with the 6–7 m beach at Bérard contain Acheulean or Levalloiso-Mousterian industries, and Neuville & Ruhlmann (1941, p. 100 n. 3) cite the discovery of 'Chellean' material in the continental deposits of the Tyrrhenian in Algeria.   [6] McBurney & Hey (1955), pp. 160–2.

[7] Neuville & Ruhlmann (1941), p. 110.

TABLE I *The older valley fill*[1]

| | Industries | | |
Local name	Within the deposit	In upper horizons	On surface
Tripolitania			
Redeposited	Aterian (b)		Neolithic
Plateau Silts (a)	Middle Palaeolithic (a)		Upper Palaeolithic (a)
Cyrenaica			
Younger Gravels (c)	Levalloisian (c)		Levalloisian (c)
Tunisia			
Limons rouges (d₁)	Aterian (d₁)	Mousterian (d₂)	
(south)			
Haute terrasse (d₂)	Mousterian and a blade industry (d₂)		
Algeria			
Mazouna Stage (f)	Mousterian (f)		
Alluvions	Aterian (w)	Ibero-Maurusian	Ibero-Maurusian
anciennes (g)	Acheulo-Mousterian (i)	(Oranian) (j)	(Oranian) (j)
Niveau III (h)			
Morocco			
Limons rouges	Micoquian (l)		
soltaniens (k)	Mousterian (m)		Ibero-Maurusian (o)
	Aterian (n)		
Spain			
Limons rouges (p)			
Alluvions rouges (q)			
Italy			
Alluvions			
terrassées (r)	Mousterian (r)		
Greece			
Red Beds (s)	Mousterian (s)	Upper Palaeolithic (t)	Neolithic 5400 B.C. (s)
Jordan			
Oberterrasse (u)	Middle and Upper Palaeolithic (v)		Kebaran (v)
Upper terrace (v)			

Note. The authority cited is not necessarily the first to describe the deposit or industry.

[1] (a) Hey (1962), p. 442; (b) McBurney & Hey (1955), pp. 225–9; (c) McBurney & Hey (1955), pp. 163–9; Hey (1962), p. 436; (d₁) Castany (1962), p. 264; (d₂) Castany (1955), p. 201; (e) Gobert (1962), p. 274; (f) Anderson (1936); (g) Gaucher (1947); (h) Boulaine (1957); (i) Vaufrey (1955), p. 101; (j) Balout (1955), p. 50; Hilly (1962), p. 361 and n. 1; (k) Choubert and others (1956); (l) Neuville & Ruhlmann (1941), p. 116; (m) Vaufrey (1955), p. 97; (n) Choubert (1962), p. 147; (o) Choubert (1962), p. 148; (p) Solé (1962), pp. 334–7; (q) Gigout (1959b), p. 1774; (r) Selli (1962) p. 411; (s) Higgs & Vita-Finzi (1966); (t) Dakaris, Higgs & Hey (1964); (u) Picard (1932), p. 230; (v) Vita-Finzi (1964); (w) Vita-Finzi (1967).

More significant is the archaeological context of the older fill. In Atlantic Morocco the *croûte calcaire supérieure* contains Acheulean remains.[1] At Gasr ed Dauun, in Tripolitania, the wadi crust incorporates a micro-Mousterian industry,[2] and, in other wadis of Tripolitania, various nondescript Middle Palaeolithic pieces. The *calcaires pulvérulents* that often underlie the crust in Atlantic Morocco (and which may be spring-laid) contain artifacts which have been described as evolved Acheulian, middle Levalloisian and Acheulo-Mousterian.[3] The true tufas of Wadi Derna (Cyrenaica) contain Levalloiso-Mousterian artifacts.[4] Arambourg termed the littoral facies of the older fill in the Maghreb and the eastern Mediterranean 'les couches rouges éluviennes à industrie levalloiso-moustérienne'.[5] In a later publication he defined the typical industry as Moustero-Aterian.[6] Table 1 shows that the latter assertion generally holds, although in some of the Jordanian wadis the fill yields a mixture of Middle and Upper Palaeolithic artifacts. In the Maghreb and in Epirus, Upper Palaeolithic industries occur in the uppermost horizons of the fill and on its surface; in Wadi Hasa (Jordan), a late Upper Palaeolithic industry, the Kebaran, occurs in a chipping floor on the older fill.[7]

Aggradation had ended by the time Capsian and Neolithic sites were occupied. The changeover from deposition to stream incision thus occurred 10,000 years ago at the earliest. Gigout places it at about 6,000 years ago in Morocco;[8] in sub-Saharan Tunisia the wadis have breached a gypsum crust which caps the Mousterian deposit and which, according to Coque,[9] formed no earlier than the ninth or tenth millennium B.C. We have seen that in the middle reaches of one Tripolitanian wadi it had not advanced far even by Roman times.

Origin of the older fill

Early accounts of alluvial terraces in the Mediterranean area favoured changes in sea-level as the controlling factor which determined whether the streams cut down or built up their beds. This (eustatic) view has survived in some quarters even though it is now abundantly clear that the major phases of alluvial deposition coincided with periods of low sea-level, the reverse of what the theory would lead one to expect. Here and there anomalous deposits have been explained

---

[1] Neuville & Ruhlmann (1941), p. 110.
[2] E. S. Higgs, personal communication. Cf. the industry of Tit Mellil in Morocco (Vaufrey 1955, pp. 78–81).
[3] Neuville & Ruhlmann (1941), p. 25; Choubert (1962), *passim*.
[4] McBurney & Hey (1955), pp. 141–59.
[5] Arambourg (1951). [6] Arambourg (1962), p. 107. [7] Vita-Finzi (1966c).
[8] Gigout (1960), pp. 83, 137. [9] Coque (1962), pp. 388–96, 419.

by localized earth movements which barred or tilted the streams. Later, the role of climatic change began to be championed on the grounds that the ice ages of higher latitudes had been echoed in the Mediterranean by 'pluvial' conditions, and hence by greater stream discharges. The various explanations that have been put forward for the deposits here equated with the older fill are based on one or more of these points of view. Now and then one meets with the suspicion that a fourth factor normally not considered for periods earlier than the Neolithic may have played some part in the shaping of the landforms known to Palaeolithic man, namely changes in the relationship between rainfall and runoff promoted by devegetation. In the days before domestication and cultivation this could have been effected by fire.

The best-known efforts to substantiate the eustatic view were made in Algeria. In 1911 de Lamothe correlated the river terraces of the Isser with the raised beaches on the coast.[1] In 1932, Anderson found a similar link between the terraces of the western Atlas rivers and the coastal succession, and attributed the deposition of the older fill (his Mazouna stage) to a sea-level 50 m higher than the present.[2] But here, as in all the littoral areas discussed in Part I, the fans of the older fill developed when the sea was markedly lower than it is now. More generally, a rising sea-level, like the erection of a reservoir, will be felt upstream only to the point where the 'backwater transition curve intersects the original stream profile', and perhaps somewhat further where the stream load consists largely of gravel; even within this distance, however, the channel may compensate for the lower gradient by an increase in depth or by some other adjustment other than aggradation.[3] In any case, the irregular longitudinal profiles of the Mediterranean valleys (as illustrated by the extreme cases of Wadis Hasnun and Turgut (Fig. 4)) would block the effects of changes in sea-level a short distance from the sea, whereas the older fill occurs as far as the uppermost headwaters—a problem which Anderson did not fail to recognize.[4]

Fluctuations of sea-level, though inadequate to explain the older fill, undoubtedly took place. Earth movements have been invoked on an *ad hoc* basis, or at best on the grounds that areas which have been mobile are likely to remain unstable: witness Vaufrey's suggestion that the Mazouna fill of Algeria, too recent to be linked with the 50 m beaches, could instead have resulted from vertical movement of the coastal ranges, which are known to have undergone post-Villafranchian folding.[5] The only supporting evidence Vaufrey adduces are variations in the elevation of the Mazouna fill.

[1] De Lamothe (1911).   [2] Anderson (1932).
[3] Leopold and others (1964), pp. 260-1.
[4] Anderson (1936), p. 375. For Algerian and Tunisian long profiles see Gautier (1911).
[5] Vaufrey (1955), p. 55.

A well-documented example of extensive recent tectonic activity on the Mediterranean littoral is that of Gafsa, in southern Tunisia, where fluvial gravels have yielded Acheulean artifacts.[1] As it is, this event antedates the deposition of the local version of the older fill, which shows no sign of disturbance and cannot be attributed to the folding, in that it is not localized upstream of the axis of uplift. Worse still, recent work by Coque has revealed that the Acheulean artifacts are not *in situ* but have been cemented in place on the surface of the folded gravels by a calcareous crust.[2] Yet it is perhaps too late to challenge what is now an established truth solidly ballasted by a weighty literature.

The one area where one might be justified in conjuring up tectonic control of stream action is the Jordan trough, for the streams that drain into it share as base-level a structural unit known to have continued moving during the Quaternary. Indeed, Quennell's views on the structural evolution of the Dead Sea Rift are based in part on reconstructed stream profiles.[3] Yet, as he himself has shown, much of the movement along the bounding faults has been horizontal. Moreover, the older fill (Upper Terrace) deposits immediately overlie the Lisan Marls, and thus postdate the major vertical movements that affected the Jordan Rift. The effects of minor changes in base-level would, like minor fluctuations in sea-level, be restricted to the lowest reaches, and could not explain aggradation throughout the length of the Jordanian valleys. Only at the head of the drainage system that enters the Jordan Rift from the east is it likely that regional tilting of the Arabia block could cause a stream to alternate from aggradation to downcutting, for it could lead to a shift in the watershed position. The resulting deposits would be equally localized.

The first clear evidence of man's interference with the natural vegetation is associated with the Capsian sites of the Maghreb, where the midden of Rammadiya at Relilaï, for example, has yielded 5,000 m³ of ashes.[4] The picture may in due course be modified by detailed palaeobotanical studies; but, as things stand, fluctuations in climate, acting directly on the landscape and indirectly through the vegetation, remain as the only acceptable mechanism for the origin of the older fill. Its detailed analysis is, however, still a matter for dispute. There are two main schools of thought: those who place the major emphasis on an increase in the transporting and eroding power of runoff, and those who think in terms of 'overloading' of the streams thanks to an increase in the supply of weathered material from the interfluves. As usual, a third, interdenominational group will probably win the day by stealing the thunder from both camps.

We have seen that the older fill includes both slope and channel deposits.

---

[1] Vaufrey (1934); Castany (1955), p. 201.   [2] Coque (1962), pp. 51–3.
[3] Quennell (1958).   [4] Balout (1955), p. 75.

Butzer has presented sedimentological evidence which suggests that alluviation in the Eurafrican subtropics is associated with increased precipitation, and that colluviation of *limons rouges* indicates prolonged, intensive rainfall within a seasonal pattern similar to that of the present,[1] or what Arambourg termed 'un intense ruissellement sous un climat chaud'.[2] Areal (as compared with linear) erosion would be promoted, with aggradation along the greater length of the streams.

Butzer recognized the possibility that cold climate weathering could have contributed to aggradation when the Würm Glacial attained its maximum severity.[3] In areas where the older fill consists predominantly of angular rock fragments, as in Cyrenaica,[4] frost-shattering would seem to have been the chief source of material. This can hardly be doubted in Morocco, where the older (or Soltanian) fill grades upstream into periglacial deposits.[5]

The flora that was present when the older fill was being laid down gives some indication of lower temperatures. For example, the Aterian site of Wadi Djouf in Algeria has yielded plant remains now characteristic of 'cooler, more mountainous' environments; the remains at the Capsian site of Relilaï correspond with species now growing 200 m higher, while those at the Upper Capsian site of 'Ain Khanga already tally with the modern plant cover.[6] Faunal remains are less helpful. Certain elements associated with Moustero-Aterian industries in the Maghreb, notably the hippopotamus and a rhinoceros (*Dicerorhinus merckii*), are absent in the Upper Palaeolithic horizons,[7] but it is difficult to evaluate the precise climatic significance of their disappearance or the relative importance of 'overkill' by hunters. Pollen studies had already suggested to many workers that cold conditions were accompanied by marked dryness, at least seasonally, and this would seem to be supported by the accumulation of manganese at various horizons in the Red Beds of Epirus.[8] The search for reliable palaeoclimatic indicators continues. Cores from the Mediterranean sea-floor at first seemed to provide the answer: the study of both isotopes[9] and fauna[10] obtained from them were thought to indicate exceptionally low temperatures some 17,000 years ago. It now appears that the former reflect the proportion of water locked up in ice bodies at a particular time while the latter was probably governed by concomitant changes in salinity.[11]

[1] Butzer (1963*a*). [2] Arambourg (1951), p. 52.

[3] Butzer (1961), p. 435; cf. (1963*b*), p. 213, where he claims that none of the deposits have been affected by periglacial processes. [4] McBurney & Hey (1955), p. 82.

[5] Choubert, Joly, Gigout, Marçais, Margat & Raynal (1956). [6] Balout (1955), p. 71.

[7] Vaufrey (1955), p. 395; Arambourg (1962), p. 107.

[8] Tippett, *in* Dakaris and others (1964), pp. 224–5.

[9] Emiliani (1955); see also Leroi-Gourhan (1963). [10] Parker (1958).

[11] Olausson (1965); Shackleton (1967).

The available evidence thus permits only the tentative conclusion that the disturbance in sediment supply/transport relationships in the Mediterranean which is indicated by the construction of steeper stream profiles during the period of the Last Glaciation was occasioned by an increase in the incidence of frost weathering in the uplands and by the seasonal incidence of more intense rains throughout the area, both of which led to a rise in the rate of interfluve erosion.

The calcareous deposits at the base of the older fill also show a degree of lithological variation which corresponds broadly with present-day climatic contrasts. Hey has already suggested that the absence of tufa in Tripolitania may be ascribed to a rainfall lower than that of Cyrenaica. In more general terms, a universal cause, which can only have been greater precipitation, was modified by local conditions to give rise to tufa where springs were thereby swollen and crusts where superficial sheetflow was induced.

Cave sequences indicate a division of the Würm sequence in the Mediterranean into a 'wet' Early Würm and a 'cold' Main Würm.[1] The alluvial deposits show that the latter was by far the more profound in its effects on the hydraulic geometry of the Mediterranean valleys.

During the rise in sea-level—the Flandrian transgression—that accompanied the waning of the Last Glacial, sedimentation took place in the estuaries, in places to a depth of over 50 m.[2] The older fill began to be eroded. The younger fill was to be laid down in the channels that now came into being.

There are traces of a phase of aggradation intermediate in age between the newer and older fills in three areas: Wadi Hasa, Jordan, where the deposit has yielded Kebaran (late Palaeolithic) artifacts and a radiocarbon age of 3,950 years;[3] coastal Tunisia, where Capsian artifacts occur both within and on a 'low terrace' which formed between the seventh and fourth millennium;[4] and the Gornalunga valley of Sicily, where aggradation took place during the Greek period.[5] For the moment these must rank as local anomalies. Other deposits, such as scree, which also date from what was predominantly an erosive interlude, do not enter into this account because they have not been subjected to a definite phase of stream processing.

[1] Butzer (1957). Biberson (1963), pp. 614–15, has suggested that the Moroccan equivalent of the Würm I of western Europe be termed *Pre-Soltanien*; the *Soltanien sensu stricto* would in this case be the equivalent of the period of maximum cold in Europe.

[2] Glangeaud & others (1952), p. 106. A world-wide rise in sea-level accompanied a complex series of climatic fluctuations towards warmer conditions between 15,000 and 7,000 years ago (Curray, 1961).

[3] Vita-Finzi (1966a).

[4] Castany (1955), p. 606; Coque (1962), p. 419.

[5] Judson (1963b).

The younger fill

The erosion of the older fill was curbed by water- and soil-conservation measures at various stages in Antiquity. As these decayed, downcutting was resumed. In the wadis of Tripolitania, Algeria and Tunisia it appears to have done so with greater effectiveness than before, and the valley crust was breached at many dam sites.

TABLE 2. *The younger valley fill*

	B.C. A.D.	500	1000	1500	1967
Tripolitania	E Roman E / dams and / walls	Roman sherds	Arab sherds	C^{14} 610	E
Cyrenaica	Greek and Roman sherds			photo / glass	E
Tunisia	E Roman E / dams	Roman sherds			E
Algeria	E Roman E / dams	Roman and Punic sherds			E
Morocco	Punic, Berber and Roman sherds	Arab sherds	C^{14} 800 C^{14} 490		E
Spain	Roman sherds	Medieval sherds			E
Italy	Roman bath	Roman sherds	C^{14} 1400 C^{14} 1140	E 1534	
Greece		Byzantine ruins	coins 565,575	Turkish midden E	
Jordan	Roman remains				E

E signifies erosion dominant in stream channels. C^{14}: radiocarbon dates for the alluvium cited in the relevant chapter. The shading indicates the maximum possible duration of stream aggradation as inferred from the relationship of the younger fill to archaeological remains.

Renewed aggradation once more resulted in steeper, more continuous longitudinal stream profiles, although the terminal gradients were less steep than those of the older fill and fan-development was less pronounced. The alluvium differs from the older fill in being predominantly buff and grey in colour and in consisting largely of silty fine sand; its gravel is subrounded or rounded and restricted to the margins and base of the deposit. Bedding is well developed.

In some areas the onset of aggradation can be dated closely, as the fill overlies

Classical buildings and dams. Otherwise we have to be content with the minimum date provided by the youngest pottery types within the alluvium. Table 2 summarizes this information. It will be noted that, in those areas where the younger fill does not overlie ancient structures, it can only be given a limiting date by reference to the youngest sherds within the deposit, and it may well be that it occurred *after* Classical times here too. Similarly, while evidence for the resumption of downcutting as early as the sixteenth century is at present restricted to Etruria,[1] there is no positive evidence that it continued beyond this date in other areas, with the exception of the headwaters of the Bel Ghadir in Cyrenaica. What is certain is that the fill was being laid down during the Middle Ages, and that it is now being eroded.

[1] Judson (1963*a*).

CHAPTER 11

LOCAL FACTORS

The accumulation of the younger fill profoundly modified the economic signifi-cance of the Mediterranean valleys. Before attempting to evaluate this change we must try to explain it. Even if a complete solution is unlikely to emerge, we may still derive from our efforts a fuller picture of the environmental changes that have taken place in the Mediterranean basin since the formation of the older fill.

In discussing the problem of geological correlation, Chamberlin wondered 'whether the earth's history is naturally divided into periodic phases of world-wide prevalence, or whether it is but an aggregation of local events dependent upon local conditions uncontrolled by overmastering agencies of universal dominance'.[1] In a study of stream processes, the term 'local' may with some justification be equated with individual drainage basins, since each of these can be viewed as a more or less self-contained dynamic system wherein the kinetic energy made available to water by elevation is dissipated.[2] The 'universal' agencies alluded to by Chamberlin evidently transcend the boundaries of the Mediterranean region, however we define it. Their consideration demands that we discover whether the events that have moulded the Mediterranean valleys are in any way unique. The adjoining areas of Europe and Africa provide ample material for a brief sortie of this kind.

In various parts of the Sahara there is geological evidence for pluvial con-ditions during the Last Glaciation of Europe, and for a less marked later moist interlude which is usually ascribed to the Neolithic.[3] In the Atakor mountains within the Hoggar massif, these two phases are represented by alluvial fills, of which the younger, 1–2 m thick and composed largely of light brown to grey silt, has yielded Neolithic pottery[4] and one sherd of historical age.[5] Rognon has found a similar deposit in Tibesti.[6] At Bou Ali (Touat) in the western Sahara, an alluvial deposit 8–10 m thick which includes marshy soils and tufa has yielded a radiocarbon date of 1520 ± 150 years near its base.[7] It is difficult not to suspect that many of the so-called 'Neolithic' deposits of the Sahara will be revealed as being entirely of historical age. In the light of what was said in chapter 5, the fact that the Guirian alluvial fill of the northwestern Sahara has been equated with the Rharbian of Morocco[8] points in this direction.

---

[1] Chamberlin (1898), quoted by Albritton (1963), p. 274.   [2] See Chorley (1962).
[3] Alimen (1963).   [4] Rognon (1967), p. 119; (1962), p. 58; cf. Dutil (1959).
[5] Rognon, personal communication, 3 May 1965.   [6] *Ibid.*
[7] Conrad (1963), p. 637.   [8] Chavaillon (1964), table 11.

At Acoris, in the Nile valley, almost two metres of well-stratified and well-assorted fine material were deposited in Coptic or early Arab times. Similar deposits were laid down at Hebenu after the Coptic period.[1] A major phase of silt deposition in the Middle Nile had taken place between about 30,000 and 10,000 years ago.[2]

On moving to Europe we encounter further parallels. In northwestern Germany, a yellow-brown sandy silt ('haugh-loam') up to 3 m thick underlies most of the valley floors. It rests unconformably on deposits dating from the Würm glaciation and others due to the Flandrian transgression, and has buried Bronze Age and medieval remains. According to Mensching it began to be laid down between the Bronze Age and early medieval times and is still being laid down today.[3] In the Rhone valley the channels cut into the alluvial cones and other deposits dating from the Würm were subsequently filled with up to 20 m of alluvium; in some places this has buried Neolithic sites.[4] According to Bourdier the deposit has an upper, yellow portion which contains both Bronze Age and historical remains.[5] He also refers to the burial of Roman and medieval remains under 4 m of alluvium in the Isère near Grenoble.[6]

Instances of historical aggradation may be found even further afield. They are commonplace, for example, in the valleys of the American west, where the trenching of a deposit laid down roughly 7,000–11,000 years ago was followed by two periods of deposition, the first somewhere between 4,000–2,200 years ago and A.D. 1100–1200 and the second between A.D. 1200–1500 and 1880 or later. The modern channels began to be cut in the late nineteenth century.[7]

To return to the Mediterranean, we have already seen that the effects of fluctuations of sea-level and of climate may be strongly modified by regional differences. Nonetheless they fall, strictly speaking, within the scope of the next chapter. In accordance with what has already been said, 'local events' include earth movements (since the basins under review lie in a variety of tectonic units) and changes in rainfall–runoff relationships produced by biotic factors. They have one immediate attraction in that, since any correlation among them is by definition the product of coincidence, discrepancies in the timing of aggradational or erosional phases in the various areas need no explanation.

If earth movements appeared wholly inadequate to explain the older fill, they are unlikely to emerge as the factor responsible for historical aggradation. But one should not fail to record the incidence of quite marked, though areally restricted, cases of uplift, depression and faulting during historical times, if only because

[1] Butzer (1959), p. 79. [2] Fairbridge (1962). [3] Mensching (1951, 1958).
[4] Bourdier (1962), p. 144. [5] Ibid. p. 344. [6] Ibid. p. 347.
[7] Martin (1963), p. 64, table 8.

they may distort the evidence relating to other geological changes. The sub-merged Greek harbour of Apollonia, in Cyrenaica, is a case in point in that it has been cited more than once as evidence of a rise of some 2 m in the level of the Mediterranean since early Classical times.[1] Recent work supports the view that the ruins, like those of the temple of Serapis at Pozzuoli, have been affected by localized movement.[2] (Conversely, the holes that riddle the columns of the Greek temples at Paestum are adequately explained by the fact that the stone em-ployed was a porous travertine,[3] without the need to invoke boring by marine organisms.)[4] Fault movement still operates at the margins of the Jordan trough but, as was noted above, it is predominantly horizontal, and at most produces offsets in the local drainage lines.[5] Finally, the rapidity with which beaches can be raised is illustrated by the uplift of part of the shore near Sidi Bou Saïd in Tunisia in 1953 to 2–3 m above its original position.[6] No clearer case for eschewing beach correlation by height could be devised; no better illustration of the localized nature of recent tectonic activity in the Mediterranean is required.

Man as geological agent

In 1859 G. P. Marsh wrote

The decay of these once flourishing [Mediterranean] countries is partly due...to that class of geological causes whose action we can neither resist nor guide, and partly also to the direct violence of hostile human force; but it is, in a far greater proportion, either the result of man's ignorant disregard of the laws of nature, or an incidental consequence of war and of civil and ecclesiastical tyranny and misrule.[7]

Before long the period of human influence on the physical landscape was elevated to the rank of Era, whether 'psychozoic', 'anthropozoic' or 'mental'.[8] In 1904 the Mental Era was thought to have just begun (although its effects seemed to be increasing 'with a rapidity quite phenomenal when measured by the slow pace of most geological change'),[9] whereas the 'Anthropogene' of some contemporary geologists extends back to 2500 B.C. or even further.[10] Thanks in part to the Dust Bowl there is now a widespread readiness to blame man for the

[1] Butzer (1958a), p. 42.
[2] Flemming (1960). This had been the view of Desio (1939, II, 53).
[3] Vita-Finzi (1966b).   [4] Gunther (1964).   [5] See, for example, Zak & Freund (1966).
[6] Castany (1953–4).   [7] Marsh (1874), p. 5; cf. Lyell (1872), I, 168–9.
[8] Glacken (1956), p. 86.
[9] Chamberlin & Salisbury (1904, quoted by Glacken 1956, p. 86).
[10] According to Bourdier (1962), p. 311, it is '[le] période où l'homme influe sur le cours de phénomènes géologiques par le déboisement' (cf. Tricart, 1953). The term has also been applied to the whole of the Quaternary in recent Russian geological literature.

vicissitudes of the soil; it has been reinforced by reaction against interpretations of history which give undue weight to the influence of climatic change.[1] Nowhere is this swing in the pendulum of culpability more evident than in the literature dealing with the Mediterranean world and the adjacent deserts and semi-deserts.[2]

It may well be chimerical to seek necessary causes in geology. But doubtless situations arise where a change in one environmental variable may precipitate an impending change. We might in such cases expect some degree of coincidence between cause (or more correctly trigger) and effect.

In Tripolitania, the history of land use may be divided into five main stages:

(i) Early agriculture, from Neolithic to Phoenician.

(ii) Roman development, begun in 46 B.C. and most advanced during the first three centuries A.D.

(iii) Agricultural decline during late Roman times and the Byzantine reconquest (534).

(iv) Widespread decay, encouraged by the Arab invasions of the seventh and eleventh centuries and by Turkish neglect.

(v) Modern development during the Italian period of colonization (1922–40) and the post-war era of foreign-aid programmes and oil revenues.

There are obvious parallels between this scheme and the alluvial chronology (see p. 44).[3] In particular, there is a strong *prima facie* case for linking the post-Classical aggradation phase with the Arab invasions, especially those of the eleventh century,[4] which, as Ibn Khaldun attested, ravaged the countryside. 'When, after the passing of Roman, Vandal and Byzantine rule, Africa fell under the sway of the Arabs, it reverted, like the Syrian lands, to very primitive conditions of life similar to those that had prevailed before its colonisation by the Carthaginians.'[5]

This is one explanation offered by Gigout for the Rharbian of Morocco: 'la pratique du nomadisme, importée par les Arabes vers le 11e siècle, a eu des effets catastrophiques sur le couvert végétal; en conséquence, l'érosion a entraîné abondamment les sols aux rivières.'[6] In the case of Olympia,[7] or of other sites

---

[1] E.g. by Huntington (1907).   [2] Shalem (1953), quoted by Monod (1958).

[3] Cf. Oldfield (1963), p. 38 (with reference to the Lake District of England): 'the ecological history deduced from the pollen analytical record, and the agricultural history reconstructed from literary evidence can be matched phase for phase and are in very close agreement throughout the whole of the post-Roman period.'   [4] Julien (1951); Golvin (1957); Gautier (1927).

[5] Rostovtseff (1957), p. 311. Yet, according to Despois (1961), p. 231, the eleventh- and twelfth-century Arab immigrations into North Africa were followed by a serious decline in population. Consequently pressure on the land was reduced, and many areas formerly cultivated may even have regained a spontaneous vegetative cover.

[6] Gigout (1960), p. 83.   [7] Philippson (1950–9), III, pt. ii, 340.

beyond the sphere of destruction of the invading nomads, responsibility tends to be transferred to the vaguer bogey of 'medieval devegetation'.

In the semi-arid areas of the western United States where detailed alluvial sequences have been established, it is generally found that, when valley alluviation affects the uppermost headwaters of a drainage system as well as the trunk streams, the bulk of the deposited material is contributed by sheet erosion and mass movement on hill-slopes and hilltops.[1] The morphological effects of unwise land use will depend on the original situation, but under certain circumstances they do consist of widespread sheet erosion and of channel aggradation a short distance downstream of the source of material.[2] It is also possible that in due course sheet erosion will expose less permeable soil horizons or bedrock, and thus yield to gullying, channel extension, and the trenching of the valley fills for which it was responsible. In other words, protracted soil erosion could conceivably give rise to a deposit such as the medieval fill of the Mediterranean and also to its subsequent incision. The waterlogging that often accompanies the accumulation of eroded soil in a flood plain could well counterfeit the effects of a change from seasonal to perennial stream flow.

The main obstacle before this interpretation of the events is one of timing. Devegetation was not a medieval innovation. It had begun in prehistory, with the need for fuel and the requirements of the chase. Later came the use of timber for houses, ships and other structures, the multiplication of grazing animals, and the clearing and tillage of land for cultivation. To these one may add wars and invasions, which often wrought the consequences described by Josephus after the destruction of Jerusalem: 'where once there had been a lovely vista of woods and parks, there was nothing but desert and the stumps of trees.'[3] In many areas the demand for timber and land rose to a peak in Classical and especially Roman times.[4] 'The *causa causarum* of the acts and neglects which have blasted with sterility and physical decrepitude the noblest half of the empire of the Caesars' was, according to Marsh, 'the brutal and exhausting despotism' of Rome as well as 'the host of temporal and spiritual tyrannies which she left as her dying curse to all her wide dominion'.[5] By the fourth century B.C., Plato was already

---

[1] Leopold and others (1964), p. 440.

[2] See, for example, Happ, Rittenhouse & Dobson (1940), p. 21.

[3] Josephus (1959), p. 303.

[4] 'The general impression left by...classical authors is that the Mediterranean lands were then more densely wooded than they are today but that already there had been considerable clearing and that the extensive forests which remained were for the most part in the mountainous areas' (Darby, 1956, p. 186). In southern Etruria, the forest cover is thought to have remained largely intact until the early fourth century B.C. (Ward Perkins, 1962, pp. 391–9). For an evaluation of Roman devegetation in Tunisia, see Despois (1961), p. 231. For general accounts of Classical deforestation, see Semple (1919) and Heichelheim (1956).   [5] Marsh (1874), p. 5.

denouncing deforestation and its evils;[1] by the end of the Republican era the Romans had stripped much of Italy.[2] Indeed the shortage and cost of timber is thought to have prompted a number of architectural innovations in Rome by the fifth century B.C.,[3] in southern Tripolitania during the fifth and sixth centuries A.D.,[4] and in the Negev during Byzantine times.[5] Yet valley aggradation is known to have occurred in Greek times only in parts of Sicily,[6] and in Roman times only in Etruria.[7]

The work of the Romans was continued with little pause. In Libya for example, the Austuriani destroyed trees and vines during the fourth century, the Leuatha and other tribes followed suit in the fifth,[8] and then yielded to the Arab 'locusts'. Yet here and there in the Mediterranean the forests and groves were spared. The Beni Hillal could not overwhelm the Berbers of the eastern Tripolitanian Gebel, while geographical isolation favoured the survival of settled agriculture in its central and western portions, to arouse the admiration of El Bekri (in the eleventh century) and of Leo Africanus (in the sixteenth).[9] Occasionally the woods survived until the late Middle Ages, the nineteenth century, or even (as in parts of Cyrenaica and Kabylie) the present day.[10] In any history of land use the breaks have more convenience than validity, and parallels between it and the geological succession may be due largely to the adoption of the same historical nomenclature for both.

It could still be argued that the effects of prehistoric and Classical clearing and cultivation were held in check by Carthaginian, Greek and especially Roman efforts at soil-conservation until these were allowed to decay. Yet, as we have seen in Algeria, Tunisia and Tripolitania, the collapse of the Roman dams was the signal for renewed stream incision, and not for aggradation.

The effects of present-day clearing, especially if followed by clean-tilled cultivation, are headward extension of drainage systems accompanied by gullying, and deposition in their lower reaches and in estuaries and deltas.

In the Tell of Oran,[11] in Algeria, torrential rains give rise to all the classic

---

[1] Plato, *Critias*, III. According to Heichelheim (1956), p. 403, Plato is unreliable, and forest estates were more extensive in Greece in Imperial Roman times than in the Classical (Greek) period.

[2] Cary (1949), p. 23. [3] Semple (1919), p. 38.

[4] Oates (1954), p. 111. [5] Woolley & Lawrence (1915), p. 53.

[6] Judson (1963*b*). [7] Judson (1963*a*).

[8] Warmington (1954), p. 26; Haynes (1955), p. 67. Enough trees remained to astound the immigrants from Egypt. (Marçais, 1946, p. 23).

[9] El Bekri (1913), pp. 19, 26; Leo Africanus (1956), 19, II.

[10] Glesinger (1960), p. 95, has estimated that 6,000 years ago there were 250–500 million acres of true forest in the Mediterranean, and that only 5 million survive. For figures regarding their distribution see Houston (1964), p. 715, appendix III. See also Lombard (1959) for timber trade in the seventh–eleventh centuries A.D. [11] Benchetrit (1954).

features of soil erosion, and the rate at which silting affects the reservoirs built in the lower reaches of the streams that drain the Tell indicates a progressive increase in its severity. Benchetrit attributes this to the removal of the forest cover that had survived until the middle of the nineteenth century as a result of a threefold increase in the native population in the twenty-five years prior to 1945. The eroded material flows to the sea, or is spread over the plains. When the Wadi Fergoug dam, erected in 1868, was broken by unusually heavy rains in 1927, the low plains of Oran received some 80,000,000 m³ of debris, which covered an area of 500 km² to a depth of 10–20 cm. In 1924, the Wadi Habra covered the plains between St Denis du Sig and Perrégaux with sediment 0·8–1 m thick.

In Tripolitania, the olive and other cultivated plants continued to decline during Turkish times, although in 1851 a fifteen-year exemption from taxes led to the planting of 30,000 olive trees in the Msellata and of 10,000 elsewhere in the Gebel.[1] In 1897 the hills of the Msellata were still relatively rich in olive groves, 'a country differing much in aspect from the bare uplands' of the rest of the Gebel[2] with their degraded steppe vegetation. The successful, though expensive, establishment of Italian farms in the Gebel Tarhuna, at Tigrinna (near Garian), and in parts of the Gefara, marked a break with the post-Roman decline. The total number of olive trees in Tripolitania rose from 450,000 to 3,800,000 between 1910 and 1944. At the same time halfa (*Stipa tenacissima*) and esparto (*Lygeum spartum*), destined chiefly for ropes and sacking and the paper mills of Scotland, began to be harvested at a far greater rate than during the preceding century.[3] This large-scale collecting was (and sometimes still is) accompanied by the belief that only drought, and not over-pulling out of season, can kill the plant, although the danger had been recognized in Algeria as early as 1889.[4] By 1920 it was said that in the country around Homs esparto had suffered so greatly in both quality and quantity that an Italian decree of 1914, which forbade esparto harvesting for four months of the year, had perhaps come too late.[5] A succession of dry years, the loss of overseas markets, and a fall in price since 1951, led to a sharp decline in the industry. But the land was not left fallow;

[1] De Leone (1960), II, 283. Many authors stress that Turkish rule in general spelled neglect rather than positive destruction. E.g. Marçais (1946), p. 305; De Mathuisieulx (1912), p. 1.

[2] Cowper (1897), p. 108.

[3] Rowland (1945), p. 119. According to Cowper (1897), p. 58, the esparto industry was started in 1868. But the Romans had referred to the area around Carthage as *campus spartarius* even though, according to Pliny, African esparto *exiguum et inutile gignitur*. Mr O. Zammit, formerly of Homs, states that thirty years ago it was not unusual for 1,300–1,400 camels loaded with esparto to come into Homs from the Tarhuna and Garian areas every day.

[4] Trotter (1915), p. 89; cf Trabut (1899) in Algeria.

[5] Dra (1955), p. 168.

some 250 km² of the better esparto land from Tarhuna to Garian have come under the plough over the last thirty years.[1] Several million trees have also been planted,[2] but outside the plantations the shrubs and trees that remain are (as in Wadi Migdal) collected for fuel. Overgrazing is equally serious, and 'attempts over the last 2,000 years to discourage free grazing by nomad livestock offer little encouragement of an early solution to this problem'.[3]

The entire character of the Gebel floods appears to have been changed by these factors in the course of recent decades. Total and peak discharges have increased markedly, and a single 100 mm storm, which in 1920 would have yielded 7–8 mm of runoff, produced about 15 mm in 1956.[4] As in the rest of the Mediterranean, gullies extend rapidly particularly where plough furrows, road drains, wheel ruts or other man-made features concentrate runoff; aggradation is localized down-valley.

The two examples of the Tell of Oran and of the Tripolitanian Gebel indicate that human activity is simply abetting the phase of downcutting that began at the close of the Last Glaciation. In the words of Buffon, 'la puissance de l'homme a secondé celle de la nature',[5] and is bringing the erosive rates for each area close to the maximum proper to its climatic regime.[6] The eroded material, by being deposited downvalley, contributes to the overall flattening of stream profiles promoted by headward erosion: the rate at which the deltas of the Po, Medjerda and Tiber have advanced may thus serve as an index of the severity of erosion inland. The principle was familiar to Pausanias:

That the Echinadian islands have not yet been joined to the mainland by the Achelous is due to the Aetolians; for they have been driven out, and the whole country has been turned into a wilderness. Hence Aetolia remaining untilled, the Achelous does not wash down so much mud on the Echinadian islands as it would otherwise do. In proof of this I can point to the Meander: flowing through the lands of Phrygia and Caria, which are

[1] Marshall (1959).
[2] Seven million trees (chiefly Australian acacia and Eucalyptus) in the winter of 1963–4 (*Sunday Ghibli*, Tripoli, 24. v. 64).
[3] Marshall (1958), p. 33.
[4] Stewart (1956), pp. 1–3.
[5] Roger (1962), p. 205; the period during which this applies is Buffon's *septième et dernière époque*. Raynal (1961), p. 564, believed that, if recent deposition resembling that which had affected the Moulouya basin were to be observed in other parts of the Mediterranean, it would be attributable to an existing climatic tendency whose 'aggressiveness' had been increased by human factors. See also Pouquet (1952), p. 297.
[6] On the slopes of the Troodos range in Cyprus, rates of sediment yield are directly related to the vegetation cover, and attain a maximum under vineyard (284 tons per square mile per annum; as compared with 44 under forest) (Burdon 1951). Various attempts have been made to determine the climatic conditions most favourable to erosion; e.g. Fournier (1960) and Langbein & Schumm (1958).

ploughed every year, it has in a short time turned the sea between Priene and Miletus into dry land.[1]

The problem remains of explaining the reversal of this trend which the Mediterranean streams experienced in the Middle Ages.[2]

[1] Pausanias (1897), VIII (vol. IVB), p. 403. Pausanias wrote in the second century A.D. Cf. Eyre (1963), p. 176, for British examples.

[2] We thus reach, by another route, Birot's conclusion with regard to the burial of Olympia that 'Ni la persistance de mouvements tectoniques, ni le déséquilibre provoqué par l'action de l'homme sur la végétation ne paraissent susceptibles de rendre compte de l'ensemble de ces phénomènes' (Birot 1964, p. 126).

CHAPTER 12

UNIVERSAL AGENCIES

As with tectonic movements, so with fluctuations of sea-level: if they proved inadequate to explain the older fill, a case for their part in shaping the younger fill hardly seems worth making.

Yet it has been made. De Lamothe, for example, suggested that the silt plain trenched by the Isser and Soummam had accumulated in response either to a change in climate or to a minor transgression.[1] More confidently, Anderson correlated the Chelif stage of Algeria with a 14 m raised beach.[2] In Morocco, as we have seen, the Rharbian phase is thought by some workers to correspond with a 2 m postglacial raised beach.[3] Occasionally the link between a rising sea-level and aggradation is only hinted at, as in the statement that the transgression which brought sea-level to its present position was accompanied and followed by a phase of aggradation which built up all the present alluvial plains.[4]

Not all are prepared to recognize the existence of a Flandrian raised beach,[5] and the issue becomes irrelevant once the Neolithic connotations of the Rharbian deposit are jettisoned, since the putative beaches are some 5,000 years too old.[6] The fact that the younger fill is of historical age also upsets any attempt to associate it with a gradual postglacial transgression. Furthermore, the level of the Mediterranean has changed little during the last 2,000 years. At Lepcis Magna there is some indication that it rose by a few centimetres between Neronian and Severan times;[7] the more dramatic traces of wave erosion which were reported on the walls of the Circus in 1912 have evaporated.[8] A raised beach near Tripoli has yielded a radiocarbon age of 1,000 years,[9] but its height of $\frac{1}{2}$ m is about the same as the present tidal range of the Mediterranean. If anything, the slow progressive rise that would seem to characterize the world's oceans must doubtless encourage estuarine and deltaic deposition. The fluctuations of the Dead Sea[10] have been equally modest and of negligible geological significance.

There remains to be considered in detail the role of historical changes in

---

[1] De Lamothe (1899), p. 280.

[2] Anderson (1936), pp. 369–70. Petrie (1928), ascribed aggradation in Wadi Ghuzzeh to 'submergence' of the coast by some 36 m.   [3] Cf. ch. 5, above, p. 60 n. 1.

[4] Birot & Dresch (1953), I, 32–3.   [5] E.g. Blanc (1962), pp. 380–1.

[6] E.g. that at Temara, dated to 5970 ± 130 years ago (Gigout, 1959a).

[7] Blanc (1958).   [8] Vinassa (1912), p. 18.   [9] Fairbridge (1958), p. 42.

[10] For recent changes see Underhill (1967).

climate. According to Brooks, 'Geological evidence by itself plays only a very small part in elucidating climatic changes during the historical period, because it is only rarely that geological deposits can be dated with sufficient accuracy'.[1] Yet even when they can their interpretation remains problematic.

By analogy with the older valley fill, the steepening of stream profiles represented by the younger fill could be ascribed to an increase in the supply of sediment to the streams prompted by areal erosion of the interfluves. But the two deposits differ in texture, degree of stratification, and colour. The younger fill is finer-grained and better sorted than the older and (in those streams that are now ephemeral) than the bedload of the modern channel. It is generally well bedded; and it is characteristically sombre in colour. It thus indicates deposition by watercourses whose regimes were less erratic than those prevailing during the earlier phase of aggradation or at the present day; at the same time it suggests that a high water-table persisted in the valley bottoms for much of the year even in the driest parts of the Mediterranean area and encouraged the survival of included plant matter.[2] The snail fauna of Wadi Kofrein, the black *tirs* and the pollen in the Rharbian deposits of 'Ain Maarouf in Morocco,[3] all point the same way. The steepening of gradients produced by aggradation may thus have served chiefly to compensate for the loss in transporting power experienced by the streams when their peak discharges were reduced.

Direct information regarding the climate of Classical times is decidedly scanty and often unhelpful (we learn, for example, that Aristotle believed Egypt was becoming drier),[4] and our faith in the few statements of fact may be undermined by their being interspersed with travellers' tales.[5] On the whole the impression gained is that climatic conditions in Roman times were not appreciably different from those of today. In Egypt, for example, the record kept by Ptolemy shows that here, in the second century A.D., the number of rainy days was about the same as now, although they may have been slightly better distributed through the year.[6] Africa's *penuria aquarum* was broken by rain for the first time in five years when Hadrian visited it.[7] Then, as now, the Mediterranean lands experienced not only prolonged droughts but also temporary and minor wetter and colder interludes, such as the period from 218 to 179 B.C.[8] Yet archaeologists working in the southern marches of Tripolitania have been forced to conclude that only some overall diminution in the annual rainfall total could account for the presence of dry *foggaras* in Fezzan[9] and for the fact that sedentary agriculture

[1] Brooks (1926), p. 335.   [2] Van Houten (1961).   [3] Choubert & Sittler (1957).
[4] Aristotle, *Meteor.* I, xiv, 351b–325a, quoted by Forbes (1963), p. 23.
[5] E.g. in Pomponius Mela, quoted by Fantoli (1933), p. 97.
[6] Brooks (1926), p. 373.   [7] McDougall (1956), p. 84.   [8] *Ibid.* p. 131.
[9] Dubief (1952).

is no longer possible in many of the wadis that had been under permanent cultivation in Roman times;[1] they claim that at first this encouraged the settlers to concentrate on the better-watered valleys, and ultimately combined with neglect and political insecurity to turn the scales in favour of their abandonment.[2] It has also been suggested that the extensive ancient terraces and works of water conservation in Tripolitania represent the efforts of the population to maintain its hold on the country in the face of progressive desiccation.[3] Such long-term trends are difficult to substantiate; but in the coastal areas, at any rate, the successful reintroduction of the olive tree during the present century shows that there has been no appreciable loss of ecological potential.

'To prove that the climate of the first century A.D. resembled that of the present day does not prove that the climate of the seventh century A.D. also resembled that of the present.'[4] For this period the shortage of precise information is exacerbated by the hazards of translation. Dozy and de Goeje,[5] for example, in commenting on Jaubert's translation of Edrisi, are at pains to stress that the life of an *homme de cabinet* is a prerequisite for such a task. Jaubert allocated fresh water to places which Edrisi said had none; he placed Barca 'on a sterile coast' where Edrisi said that it 'combines trade by land with maritime trade'; he mistook the term 'perennial' for the name of a stream. Nonetheless certain divergences from the present are well substantiated. Braudel lists the floods and frosts that afflicted Italy, France and the Balkans towards the end of the sixteenth century.[6] Huntington and Visher found signs of 'climatic stress' during the fourteenth.[7] Butzer's 'Postpluvial IV b', which extended from A.D. 700 to about 1900, was characterized by somewhat higher rainfall and colder winters than previously or since,[8] and found an echo in the high stands of the Caspian between the ninth and tenth and the seventeenth and nineteenth centuries A.D.[9]

It would indeed be surprising to find no trace in the Mediterranean of the 'Little Ice Age' which affected western Europe between A.D. 1550 and 1850, or of the warm epoch ('Little Optimum') of A.D. 1000–1200.[10] During the former the European depression tracks lay 5–10° south of their present path[11] and probably meant an increase in the number of rain-bearing depressions that reached the Mediterranean.[12] The Little Optimum may have had a similar effect

---

[1] Goodchild & Ward Perkins (1949), p. 95.
[2] Reynolds & Ward Perkins (1952), p. 217; Goodchild (1950), p. 174.
[3] Myres (1910), p. 679.
[4] Brooks (1926), p. 327.
[5] Dozy & De Goeje (1866), pp. vii–viii and *passim*.
[6] Braudel (1949), pp. 233–5. See also Lamb (1963), p. 128.
[7] Huntington & Visher (1922), p. 87 and 109.
[8] Butzer (1958a), p. 128. [9] Butzer (1958b), p. 138.
[10] Lamb (1964), p. 336; Le Roy Ladurie (1965). [11] Lamb (1964), pp. 336–7. [12] Lamb (1963), p. 145.

in winter and also increased the incidence of summer rains.[1] A change in the seasonal pattern of precipitation would have been more significant than one in annual totals: in areas where the vegetation cover protects the soil incompletely, changes in the number, duration and timing of rains of different sizes and intensities can have profound effects on the erosive power of runoff and on stream regimes.[2]

To sum up, a climatic interpretation of historical aggradation in the Mediterranean is favoured by its incidence from France to the Hoggar and from Palestine to Morocco, by the knowledge that medieval Europe experienced a minor Ice Age and other prolonged periods of anomalous climate, and by the inadequacy of other explanations. The development of the older fill seemingly in response to climatic changes in areas as diverse as those encompassed by this study shows that their streams can react in similar manner and more or less simultaneously. Little more than this can be said until a better understanding of the relationship between modern hydrological regimes and stream geometry makes it possible to interpret past stream morphology in terms of discharges, regimes and ultimately climate.

[1] *Ibid.*
[2] Leopold (1951).

CHAPTER 13

IMPLICATIONS

While many obstacles hinder any attempt to lay bare the mechanism that has moulded the Mediterranean valleys, implications of their metamorphosis are immediately apparent.

In the Introduction, one historian's faith in the permanence of the landscape of Antiquity was queried. We are now better equipped to face the issue. The words of H. A. L. Fisher will serve to restate it.

In the last three thousand years there has been little change in the geographical conformation or climatic conditions of Europe. Here and there the sea has gained upon the land, or the land encroached upon the sea. Here and there a harbour has been silted up, a river has changed its course, a hill has subsided. But the broad currents of history have not been and could not be altered by such slight changes as these.[1]

The valleys, it will be agreed, have changed more than somewhat. Whether the 'broad currents of history' will have been altered as a result is for historians to decide. The paragraphs that follow are intended to draw attention to some of the side effects of geological change that seem to merit their consideration.

A consequence of widespread alluviation which is obvious enough to have escaped general notice is the obliteration of ancient remains in areas where one might expect them to pullulate. Despois, struck by the rapidity of contemporary flood deposition, suggested that it could explain the absence of water-control structures and other vestiges of Roman occupation in parts of lowland Tunisia.[2] In the Chelif valley of Algeria, where post-Roman aggradation has been extensive, it has occasioned the theory that saline soils or lack of water inhibited Roman settlement in areas which otherwise seem well suited to agricultural development.[3] One is led to wonder whether the role of malaria and other obstacles to settlement in the past may not have been exaggerated in a similar way where the search for sites, though thorough, has remained literally superficial. Attempts to redraw the map of Classical or medieval times[4] cannot fail to benefit from acknowledging this possibility.

Burial under river alluvium is, of course, a common fate for archaeological sites. The Mediterranean sequence is of broader significance in showing that

[1] Fisher (1965), I, 19.
[2] Despois (1955), pp. 101 n. 3 and 119. The role of wind may be given undue weight in attempts to explain the movement of soil downhill. See, for example, Fries (1962), p. 246.
[3] Boulaine (1957), pp. 87–9.   [4] E.g. Dussaud (1927).

116

extraordinary local circumstances are not always necessary to bring this about. The muds that entombed Mohenjo-Daro and Sybaris may well have been ponded by localized earth movements;[1] yet deposits not much less extensive than those of the Indus and the Crati accumulated in the space of a few centuries seemingly without the help of sub-crustal forces. In some respects the situation represents a survival of the conflict between the Catastrophist and Uniformitarian philosophies which split geology in the nineteenth century.[2] The realization that agencies now in operation could, given sufficient time, produce many of the features recorded in the geological column did not do away with catastrophic occurrences, but it did cut down on the number that were necessary.

In the Mediterranean valleys, alluviation took on major proportions in two situations: when channel erosion upvalley led to aggradation downstream, and when channel steepening involved channel filling from the headwaters to the coast (Fig. 43). In the last two millennia, and indeed since the retreat of the Würm ice sheets, the former tendency has predominated. Hence, if this account has a message for the conservationist (as well as the historian), it is that the phase of soil erosion which now afflicts the Mediterranean basin represents a return to 'normality', and that measures intended to restrain it act, in a sense, against nature. It is worth adding that, although the Romans fully deserve to be regarded as conservation-minded, their most successful schemes benefited from the fruits of soil erosion: the soil-retention dams and terraces of North Africa did not halt erosion, but trapped and concentrated material washed down from the hills in units which were easy to cultivate and to irrigate. *Natura non nisi parendo vincitur.*

Yet it would be misguided to urge a wholesale return to the agricultural methods of Antiquity.[3] Considerations of economics apart, the changes undergone by the valleys are profound and sometimes irreversible. On the deficit side we find the soils that could once be watered by flood-diversion have been washed away, the crusts on which the dams were built have been breached, the reserves of soil from the hilltops have been depleted. On the credit side we have the medieval alluvial fill and the expanded deltas, whose existence in Antiquity would surely have taken the sting out of the legend of the Elysian Fields.[4]

A convenient frame of reference for evaluating the latent economic significance of these changes is provided by Van Bath in his study of the agrarian history of medieval Europe,[5] where he considers the interplay of four major 'external

[1] Raikes (1967), pp. 179 and 182.
[2] See Daniel (1950) and Chorley and others (1964), *passim*.
[3] For accounts of the reconstruction of ancient farms in the Negev, see Evenari and others (1963).
[4] Vita-Finzi (1966a); Cary (1949), p. 42.
[5] Van Bath (1963), p. 9.

factors': Environment (E), Population (P), Exploited Area (A), and Farming Technique and Knowledge (F). In his opinion, E and to some extent A are, in the case of western Europe, fairly constant quantities. Climatic changes, for example, do not seem adequate to explain the 'periodic ups and downs' experienced by its economic life since 1200;[1] and, though land has been gained by reclamation and lost through flooding or wind erosion,[2] the key factors remain population and technology.

The point at which exploitable area is actually exploited is clearly a matter of technology. If we confine our attention to total available land, we find that the accumulation of both the older and the younger fills of the Mediterranean signified distinct gains for the valleys at the expense of older deposits and of isolated pockets of soil in the uplands. Like the soil-retention dams, these two phases led to the concentration of dispersed soil material, a gain not fully realized until the introduction of mechanization, but nonetheless a gain. With certain exceptions these fills furnished the Mediterranean lands with most of their *terre végétale*, to use the term applied to the fertile uppermost alluvium of lower Egypt laid down in the course of the last 10,000 years.[3]

The earliest attempts at agriculture coincide broadly with the completion of the older fill. In Jordan, Wadi Hasa was even more obliging in providing ideal conditions for flood irrigation.[4] In slope the surface of the older fill ranged from the angle of rest of angular scree to horizontality along the valley axes. How far steep gradients hampered early cultivators is not known; the Roman agronomists make little mention of this problem, and then only in passing.[5] As regards soil texture, the admixture of gravel and sand in the course of deposition was beneficial to primitive cultivation where the fines were derived largely from pockets of heavy *terra rossa*. The main limitation to the exploitation of the older fill was probably lack of irrigation water, for it was restricted to rainfall, to the ephemeral floods contributed by the tributaries from which the lateral fans emerged, and to occasional valley-side springs. The marginal character of agriculture under such circumstances is brought out in parts of modern Epirus, where older fill terraces on opposite sides of the same valley sometimes contrast markedly in agricultural prosperity, apparently because aspect, and thus evaporation, spells the difference between sufficient and insufficient moisture.

In parts of Jordan, Roman irrigation canals made it possible to water portions of the older fill downvalley. But, above the reach of floods and of diversion or storage schemes based on them, the limits that prevailed at the close of the

---

[1] Van Bath (1963), p. 8.   [2] *Ibid.* pp. 160–2.
[3] Hayes (1964), pp. 81.   [4] Vita-Finzi (1966*c*).
[5] E.g. Varro, *De re rustica* 1. 18. 4. (I am indebted to Prof. K. D. White for this reference.)

Palaeolithic continued to operate. This fact should colour statements such as that by Heichelheim:

[In] the Ancient Orient...the floods of the Nile, the Euphrates [etc.]...fertilised..the land annually without man's help...The districts which the water did not reach, the coastal regions, and the lands round the oases of the Aegean region and Palestine...could only be used by man with the aid of constant and careful irrigation. By these means these marginal lands became fertile and cultivated, often better than to-day.[1]

The post-Classical alluvia that form the larger part of the Mediterranean valley floors would provide a teleologist with even better ammunition than the flood-deposits of Wadi Hasa. Gently sloping and smooth, loamy in texture, and low enough to be irrigated with ease, they came into being ripe for development or, at the worst, marred by excess moisture which drainage could easily cure.[2]

These virtues add up to an appreciable improvement in the agricultural potential of the Mediterranean lands (from the point of view of present-day techniques of land use)[3] since Classical times, in complete opposition to the resilient and still widespread belief in the physical decay of the Ancient World. Geology is less explicit about the climatic aspects of Van Bath's variable E. Yet, if we accept the information it yields in a partially decoded state, namely in terms of hydrology, we can glean certain facts which are more relevant to economic history than wind speeds or mean annual temperature.

Stream behaviour in Classical times was much like that of today; if anything, the streams suffered somewhat less violent fluctuations in discharge from season to season. During the Middle Ages the valley floors were being built up by silt-laden floods. The literary evidence bears witness to this state of affairs. The geographer Ibn Said, quoting an account by Abou El Feddah, compared the Chelif with the Nile in that it replenished the fertility of its valley by periodic flooding;[4] by 1846 stream incision must have supervened, for Christian could see no reason for El Feddah's comparison.[5] El Bekri drew a similar analogy between the Nile and the Ziz of southern Morocco,[6] where today the image would seem fanciful.

The reputations of medieval farmers as well as those of the geographers may be restored by the geological record. The spread of marshy conditions in the

---

[1] Heichelheim (1958), p. 91.

[2] As in the Arta Plain of Greece, drained this century (Admiralty, 1945, (Greece) pp. 3, 27).

[3] Most of the agricultural land used by the villagers of Fuentenueva, on the Ebro, is provided by the younger fill. In February 1964 a farmer stated that these soils were so clayey that five horses were needed to pull a plough when three could manage on the lighter soils of the older fill. Where tractors are employed the younger fill comes into its own since it is easily irrigated and gives good yields under grain, while the older fill is relegated to vines.

[4] Boulaine (1957), p. 91.   [5] Ibid. p. 91, n. 15.   [6] Dozy & De Goeje (1866), p. 70.

Roman Campagna in the early Middle Ages could have followed the neglect of drainage systems,[1] but it could also be one of the negative aspects of aggradation. Instances of social and economic decline which have been attributed to the Black Death may, as Lamb suggests, be linked to climatic deterioration;[2] this in turn could have operated through the medium of changes in stream behaviour. In the Mediterranean, the most prominent example of medieval 'deterioration' was equivalent to a reduction in the power of the streams to export sediment from their basins. For later centuries this was, if anything, a boon.

[1] Frank (1933–40), pp. 4–11, quoted by Cary (1949), p. 128 n. 4.
[2] Lamb (1965), p. 15.

APPENDIX

A sample of the charcoal from the lower terrace in Wadi Ganima (see p. 37) was submitted to Dr C. R. Metcalfe, Royal Botanic Gardens, Kew, who kindly reported as follows:

The sample of charcoal which you submitted has been examined very thoroughly, and, as far as we can determine, the whole of it is derived from one, or at most two, kinds of wood. Of the species that are known to occur at the present time in the locality from which your sample was obtained, your charcoal agrees most closely with *Maerua crassifolia*, which is a member of the family Capparidaceae. The individual fragments in your sample show rather a wide range of variation particularly in the distribution of the vessels, but, as far as we can judge, the wood of *Maerua crassifolia* exhibits a similar range of structural variation. Other species of *Maerua* are also known to occur in the same locality, but these are believed to be much less common and the plants are also smaller and less vigorous in growth, so on these grounds they seem less likely to be the source of the charcoal.

There is also another plant, *Capparis spinosa*, belonging to the same family as *Maerua crassifolia*, of which the wood structure is very similar. This species also occurs in the same locality. Unfortunately we have very little reference material of this species and for this reason it has not been possible to compare it very thoroughly with your charcoal. On the whole we think *Capparis spinosa* is less likely to be the correct species. A third possibility is that your sample might contain a mixture of both species.

REFERENCES

Admiralty (1941 and 1942). *Morocco*. Naval Intelligence Division. Geographical Handbooks. London. (2 vols.)

Admiralty (1941, 1942, 1944). *Spain and Portugal*. Naval Intelligence Division. Geographical Handbooks. London. (3 vols.)

Admiralty (1943). *Palestine and Transjordan*. Naval Intelligence Division. Geographical Handbooks. London.

Admiralty (1943 and 1944). *Algeria*. Naval Intelligence Division. Geographical Handbooks. London. (2 vols.)

Admiralty (1944). *Italy*. Naval Intelligence Division. Geographical Handbooks. London. (3 vols.)

Admiralty (1944 and 1945). *Greece*. Naval Intelligence Division. Geographical Handbooks. London. (3 vols.)

Admiralty (1945). *Tunisia*. Naval Intelligence Division. Geographical Handbooks. London.

Albritton, C. C. (1963). Philosophy of geology: a selected bibliography and index, *in* C. C. Albritton (ed.), *The fabric of geology*. Reading, Mass., pp. 262–363.

Alimen, H. (1963). Considérations sur la chronologie du Quaternaire saharien. *Bull. Soc. géol. Fr.* (7), **5**, 627–34.

Almagià, R. (1907, 1910). Studi geografici sulle frane in Italia. *Mem. Soc. geogr. ital.* **13** and **14**.

Ambroggi, R. and others (1952). Hydrogéologie du Maroc. *XIX Int. Geol. Cong., Mon. reg. sér. 3: Maroc no. 4.* Rabat.

Anderson, R. van V. (1932). The Pleistocene Mazouna stage in western Algeria, containing artifacts. *Bull. geol. Soc. Amer.* **43**, 847–74.

Anderson, R. van V. (1936). Geology in the coastal Atlas of western Algeria. *Mem. geol. Soc. Amer.* **4**. Washington.

Arambourg, C. (1951). Les limites et les corrélations du Quaternaire africain. *XVII Int. Geol. Cong., London, sec. K*, pt. XI, 49–54.

Arambourg, C. (1962). Les faunes mammalogiques du Pléistocène circumméditerranéen. *Quaternaria* **6**, 97–109.

Aubouin, J., Brunn, J. H., Celet, P., Dercourt, J., Godfriaux, I. & Mercier, J. (1963). Esquisse de la géologie de la Grèce, *in* M. Durand Delga (ed.), *Livre à la mémoire du Professeur Paul Fallot*. 2 vols. *Mém. h.-sér, Soc. géol. France*.

Awad, H. (1963). Some aspects of the geomorphology of Morocco related to the Quaternary climate. *Georgr. J.* **129**, 129–39.

Balout, L. (1955). *Préhistoire de l'Afrique du Nord*. Paris.

Baradez, J. (1949). *Fossatum Africae*. Paris.

Barth, H. (1857). *Travels and discoveries in North and Central Africa* (2nd ed.). London.

Beaudet, G., Destombes, J., Jeannette, A. & Maurer, G. (1960). Recherches géologiques et morphologiques sur le quaternaire de la Meseta côtière atlantique marocaine entre Fédala, Bouznika et Boulhaut. *Notes marocaines (Soc. Géogr. Maroc)*, no. 13, 5–33.

Beaudet, G., Jeannette, A. & Mazéas, J. P. (1964). Les dépôts quaternaires du bas oued Tensift (Maroc occidental). *Rev. Géogr. maroc.* no. 5, 35–61.

Beaudet, G. & Maurer, G. (1960). Note préliminaire sur les basses terrasses grises des vallées exoréiques du Maroc. *Notes marocaines (Soc. Géogr. Maroc)*, no. 13, 45–50.

Beaudet, G. & Maurer, G. (1961). Dépôts et morphogenèse quaternaires dans la vallée inférieure de l'oued Lao. *Notes marocaines (Soc. Géogr. Maroc)* no. 15, 13–25.

Benchetrit, M. (1954). L'érosion accélérée dans les chaines telliennes d'Oranie. *Rev. Géom. Dyn.* **5**, 145–67.

REFERENCES

Bennett, H. H. (1960). Soil erosion in Spain. *Geogr. Rev.* **50**, 59–72.

Béquignon, Y. (1937). *La vallée du Spercheios des origines au IVe siècle.* Paris.

Berthelot, A. (1927). *L'Afrique saharienne ce qu'en ont connu les anciens.* Paris.

Biberson, P. (1961). *Le cadre paléogéographique de la préhistoire du Maroc atlantique.* Rabat.

Biberson, P. (1963). Quelques précisions sur les classifications du quaternaire marocain. *Bull. Soc. géol. Fr.* (7) **5**, 607–16.

Birot, P. (1964). *La Méditerranée et le Moyen Orient:* I (2nd ed., revised). Paris.

Birot, P. & Dresch, J. (1953 and 1956). *La Méditerranée et le Moyen Orient.* Paris. (2 vols.)

Blanc, A. C. (1958). Una formazione di 'Trottoir' post-romana a ridosso del Tempio di Nettuno a Leptis Magna, *in* R. Bartoccini (1958), *Il porto romano di Leptis Magna.* Boll. Centro Studi per la Storia dell'Architettura, no. 13, suppl. Rome.

Blanc, A. C. (1962). Sur le Pliocène marin des côtes tyrrhéniennes et ioniennes et les cultures paléolithiques associées. *Quaternaria* **6**, 371–89.

Boulaine, J. (1957). *Étude sur les sols des plaines du Chélif.* Alger.

Bourdier, F. (1962). *Le bassin du Rhône au Quaternaire.* Paris. (2 vols.)

Bowen, R. Le B., Jr. & Albright, F. P. (1958). *Archaeological discoveries in south Arabia.* Baltimore.

Bradford, J. (1957). *Ancient landscapes.* London.

Braudel, F. (1949). *La Méditerranée et le monde méditerranéen à l'époque de Philippe II.* Paris.

Brogan, O. (1965). The Roman remains in the Wadi el-Amud. *Libya Antiqua* **1**, 47–56.

Brooks, C. E. P. (1926). *Climate through the ages.* London.

Broughton, T. R. S. (1929). *The Romanisation of Africa Proconsularis.* Baltimore.

Bryan, K. (1954). *The geology of Chaco Canyon, New Mexico.* Washington.

Burdon, D. J. (1951). The relationship between erosion of soil and silting of reservoirs in Cyprus. *Jour. Inst. civ. Engrs* **7**, 662–85.

Burdon, D. J. (1959). *Handbook of the geology of Jordan.* Colchester.

Burollet, P. F. (1952). *Porto Farina. Carte géologique de la Tunisie, Feuille No. 7 (Notice explicative).* Tunis.

Burollet, P. F. (1952–3). Méandres anciens et nouveaux dans la région de Souk el Arba. *Bull. Soc. Sci. nat. Tunis* **6**, 57–9.

Burollet, P. F. (1956). *Contribution à l'étude stratigraphique de la Tunisie Centrale.* Tunis.

Butler, H. C. (1920). Desert Syria, the land of a lost civilization. *Geogr. Rev.* **9**, 77–108.

Butler, S. (1897). *The authoress of the Odyssey.* London.

Butzer, K. W. (1957). Mediterranean pluvials and the general circulation of the Pleistocene. *Geogr. Annlr* **39**, 48–53.

Butzer, K. W. (1958a). *Quaternary stratigraphy and climate in the Near East.* Bonn.

Butzer, K. W. (1958b). Russian climate and the hydrological budget of the Caspian Sea. *Rev. canad. Géogr.* **12**, 129–39.

Butzer, K. W. (1959). Some recent geological deposits in the Egyptian Nile valley. *Geogr. J.* **125**, 75–9.

Butzer, K. W. (1961). Paleoclimatic implications of Pleistocene stratigraphy in the Mediterranean area. *Ann. N.Y. Acad. Sci.* **95**, 449–56.

Butzer, K. W. (1963a). Climatic–geomorphologic interpretation of Pleistocene sediments in the Eurafrican subtropics, *in* F. C. Howell & F. Bourlière (eds.), *African ecology and human evolution.* London, pp. 1–27.

Butzer, K. W. (1963b). The last 'pluvial' phase of the Eurafrican subtropics, *in Changes of Climate,* UNESCO Arid Zone Research XX, Paris, pp. 211–21.

Butzer, K. W. (1964). *Environment and archeology.* London.

Camps, G. (1955). Le gisement atérien du Cap Franchet d'Esperey (Arzew). *Libyca. Série anthrop. arch. préhist.* **3**, 17–56.

Caputo, G. (1951). Scavi Sahariani (II). *Mon. Ant. Accad. Naz. Lincei* **41**, 150–242.

Cary, M. (1949). *The geographic background to Greek and Roman history.* Oxford.

REFERENCES

Castany, G. (1952). Atlas Tunisien oriental et Sahel. *XIX Int. Geol. Cong., Mon. reg. sér. 2: Tunisie no. 6*. Tunis.

Castany, G. (1953–4). Mouvements actuels de terrains à Sidi bou Saïd. *Bull. Soc. Sci. nat. Tunis* **7**, 57–60.

Castany, G. (1955). Plissements quaternaires dans la région de Gafsa et le sud Tunisien. *Geol. Rdsch.* **43**, 196–203.

Castany, G. (1962). Le Tyrrhénien de la Tunisie. *Quaternaria* **6**, 229–69.

Célérier, J. & Charton, A. (1924). Profils en long des cours d'eau marocains. *Ann. Géogr.* **33**, 286–96.

Charles-Picard, G. (1959). *La civilisation de l'Afrique romaine*. Paris.

Chavaillon, J. (1964). *Étude stratigraphique des formations quaternaires du Sahara nord-occidental*. Paris.

Choisy, A. (1873). *L'art de bâtir chez les Romains*. Paris.

Chorley, R. J. (1962). Geomorphology and general systems theory. *U.S. Geol. Survey Prof. Paper 500 B*.

Chorley, R. J., Dunn, A. J. & Beckinsale, R. P. (1964). *The history of the study of landforms*, 1. London.

Choubert, G. (1955). Note sur la géologie des terrains récents des Doukkala. *Notes Mém. Serv. Mines Carte géol. Maroc* XIII, no. 128, 9–46.

Choubert, G. (1962). Réflexion sur les parallélismes probables des formations quaternaires atlantiques du Maroc avec celles de la Méditerranée. *Quaternaria* **6**, 137–75.

Choubert, G., Joly, F., Gigout, M., Marçais, J., Margat, J. & Raynal, R. (1956). Essai de classification du quaternaire continental du Maroc. *C.R. Acad. Sci., Paris* **243**, 504–6.

Choubert, G. & Sittler, C. (1957). Les terrasses de l'Aïn Maarouf et la microflore sporo-pollinique de ses dépôts néolithiques (Région d'el Hajeb, Maroc). *Bull. Carte géol. Als. Lorr.* **10**, 151–2.

Christie, A. M. (1955). *Geology of the Garian area*. UN, New York.

Conrad, G. (1963). Degré d'évolution des sédiments néolithiques et post-néolithiques du Touat. Comparaison avec le Saoura. *Bull. Soc. géol. Fr.* (7), **5**, 635–44.

Coque, R. (1962). *La Tunisie présaharienne*. Paris.

COTHA (1954 a). *Wadi Megenin: Rapport général*. Grenoble.

COTHA (1954 b). *Aménagement de quelques uadis de la Gefara*. Grenoble.

COTHA (1956 a). *Caam wadi development scheme: geologic and topographic survey for a storage dam site*. Grenoble.

COTHA (1956 b). *Aménagement de l'Uadi Caam. Campagne de mesures hydrologiques 1955–56*. Grenoble.

COTHA (1957). *Aménagement de l'Uadi Caam. Campagne de mesures hydrologiques 1956–7*. Grenoble.

Cowper, H. S. (1897). *The Hill of the Graces*. London.

Curray, J. R. (1961). Late Quaternary sea level: a discussion. *Bull. geol. Soc. Amer.* **72**, 1707–12.

Dakaris, S. I., Higgs, E. S. & Hey, R. W. (1964). The climate, environment and industries of Stone Age Greece. I. *Proc. Prehist. Soc.* **30**, 199–244.

Daniel, G. E. (1950). *A hundred years of archaeology*. London.

Darby, H. C. (1956). The clearing of the woodland in Europe, *in* W. L. Thomas (ed.), *Man's role in changing the face of the earth*. Chicago, pp. 183–216.

D'Arrigo, A. (1956). *Natura e tecnica nel mezzogiorno*. Florence.

De Lamothe, L. J. B. (1899). Note sur les anciennes plages et terrasses du bassin de l'Isser (Département d'Alger) et de quelques autres bassins de la côte algérienne. *Bull. Soc. géol. Fr.* **27** (s. 3), 257–303.

De Lamothe, L. J. B. (1911). Les anciennes lignes de rivage du Sahel d'Alger. *Mém. Soc. géol. Fr.* (4) 1.

De Leone, E. (1960). *La colonizzazione dell'Africa del nord*. Padua. (2 vols.)

Demangeot, J. (1956). L'évolution quaternaire des côtes de Cyrénaïque. *Bull. Soc. Géogr. Égypte*, **29**, 33–42.

De Mathuisieulx, E.-M. (1912). *La Tripolitaine d'hier ct de demain*. Paris.

REFERENCES

Desio, A. (1934, 1935, 1939). *Missione scientifica della Reale Accademia d'Italia a Cufra (1931*–IX). Rome. (3 vols.)

Despois, J. (1935). *Le Djebel Nefousa*. Paris.

Despois, J. (1955). *La Tunisie orientale—Sahel et Basse Steppe* (2nd ed.). Paris.

Despois, J. (1961). Development of land use in Northern Africa, with references to Spain, *in* L. D. Stamp (ed.), *History of land use in arid regions*. UNESCO Arid Zone Research XVII, Paris, pp. 219–37.

Despois, J. & Raynal, R. (1967). *Géographie de l'Afrique du nord-ouest*. Paris.

Dörpfeld, W. (1935). *Alt-Olympia*. Berlin.

Dozy, R. & De Goeje, M. J. (1866). *Description de l'Afrique et de l'Espagne par Edrisi*. Leiden.

Dra, M. (1955). Egypt, Eritrea, Libya and the Sudan, *in Plant Ecology. Reviews of Research*. UNESCO, Arid Zone Research VI, Paris, pp. 131–94.

Dresch, J. (1941). *Recherches sur l'évolution du relief dans le Massif Central du Grand Atlas—le Haouz et le Sous*. Tours.

Dresch, J. and others (1952). Aspects de la géomorphologie du Maroc. *XIX Int. Geol. Cong., Mon. Reg. sér. 3: Maroc no. 3*. Casablanca.

Dubief, J. (1952). *Report on the evolution of arid zones in the past and today*. UNESCO, Paris.

Durand, J.-H. (1959). *Les sols rouges et les croûtes en Algérie*. Algiers.

Dussaud, R. (1927). *Topographie historique de la Syrie antique et médiévale*. Paris. *Bibliothéque archéologique et historique*. Tome 4.

Dutil, P. (1959). Sur la présence de deux niveaux quaternaires dans le massif central du Sahara (Hoggar). *C.R. Soc. géol. Fr.* pp. 199–200.

El Bekri (1913). *Description de l'Afrique Septentrionale* (tr. M. G. de Slane). Algiers.

Emiliani, C. (1955). Pleistocene temperature variations in the Mediterranean. *Quaternaria* 2, 87–98.

Evenari, M., Shanan, L. & Tadmor, N. H. (1963). Runoff-farming in the Negev desert of Israel. Progress Report on the Avdat and Shivta farm projects for the years 1958–1962. *Spec. Publ. Nat. Univ. Ints. Agric., Rehovot*, no. 393-A.

Evenari, M., Shanan, L., Tadmor, N. & Aharoni, Y. (1961). Ancient agriculture in the Negev. *Science* 133, 979–96.

Eyre, S. R. (1963). *Vegetation and soils, a world picture*. London.

Fairbridge, R. W. (1958). Dating the latest movements of the Quaternary sea-level. *Trans. N.Y. Acad. Sci.* 20, 471–82.

Fairbridge, R. W. (1962). New radiocarbon dates of Nile sediments. *Nature, Lond.* 196, 108–10.

Fantoli, A. (1933). *La Libia negli scritti degli antichi*. Rome.

Fantoli, A. (1952). *Le pioggie della Libia*. Rome.

Fisher, H. A. L. (1965). *A history of Europe*. (2 vols.) (6th impression, first published 1935.) London.

Flemming, N. C. (1960). Apollonia Expedition Report 1958–9 (unpublished).

Floridia, G. B. (1939). Osservazioni sul Miocene dei dintorni di Homs. *Boll. Soc. geol. ital.* 58, 245–60.

Forbes, R. J. (1963). *Studies in ancient technology*, VII. Leiden.

Fossombroni, V. (1823). *Memorie idraulico-storiche sopra la Val-di-Chiana*, I (2nd ed.). Bologna.

Fournier, M. F. (1960). *Climat et érosion*. Paris.

Franchetti, L. (1914). *La Missione Franchetti in Tripolitania: il Gebel*. Florence.

Fries, C. (1962). Forest and soil in Etruria, *in* A. Boëthius, C. Fries and others, *Etruscan culture—land and people*. New York and Malmö.

Gardiner, E. N. (1925). *Olympia, its history and remains*. Oxford.

Gaucher, G. (1947). Les dépôts quaternaires du Bas-Chélif et des basses plaines oranaises. *C.R. Acad. Sci., Paris* 225, 65–6.

Gauckler, P. (1897). *Enquête sur les installations romaines en Tunisie*. Paris.

Gautier, E. F. (1911). Profils en long de cours d'eau en Algérie-Tunisie. *Ann. Géogr.* 20, 351–66, 431–47.

REFERENCES

Gautier, E. F. (1927). *L'Islamisation de l'Afrique du Nord. Les siècles obscurs du Maghreb.* Paris.

Gigout, M. (1957). Recherches sur le Quaternaire marocain. *Trav. Inst. scient. chérif., Sér. géologie et géographie physique*, no. 7. Rabat.

Gigout, M. (1959*a*). Âges, par radiocarbone, de deux formations des environs de Rabat (Maroc). *C.R. Acad. Sci., Paris* **249**, 2802–3.

Gigout, M. (1959*b*). À propos du Quaternaire sur le littoral des provinces du Levant espagnol. Quaternaire continental. *C.R. Acad. Sci., Paris* **249**, 1774–6.

Gigout, M. (1960). Nouvelles recherches sur le Quaternaire marocain et comparaisons avec l'Europe. *Trav. Lab. Géol. Univ. Lyon (n.s.)* **6**.

Glacken, C. J. (1956). Changing ideas of the habitable world, *in* W. L. Thomas (ed.) (1956), *Man's role in changing the face of the earth*. Chicago, pp. 70–92.

Glangeaud L. and others (1952). Histoire géologique de la province d'Alger. *XIX Int. Geol. Cong., Mon. reg. sér. 1: Algérie no. 25*. Algiers.

Glesinger, E. (1960). The Mediterranean project. *Sci. Amer.* **207**, 86–103.

Gobert, E. G. (1962). La préhistoire dans la zone littorale de la Tunisie. *Quaternaria* **6**, 271–307.

Goblot, H. (1963). Dans l'ancien Iran, les techniques de l'eau et la grande Histoire. *Annales. Économies, sociétés, civilisations* **18**, 500–20.

Golvin, L. (1957). *Le Maghrib central à l'époque des Zirides*. Paris.

Goodchild, R. G. (1949). *Reports and monographs of the Department of Antiquities in Tripolitania* II. Tripoli.

Goodchild, R. G. (1950). Roman Tripolitania: reconnaissance in the desert frontier zone. *Geogr. J.* **115**, 161–78.

Goodchild, R. G. (1952*a*) Farming in Roman Libya. *Geogr. Mag.* **25**, 70–80.

Goodchild, R. G. (1952*b*). The decline of Libyan agriculture. *Geogr. Mag.* **25**, 141–56.

Goodchild, R. (1959). *Cyrene and Apollonia*. Antiquities Department of Cyrenaica.

Goodchild, R. G. & Ward Perkins, J. B. (1949). The *Limes Tripolitanus* in the light of recent discoveries. *J. Roman Stud.* **39**, 81–95.

Goodchild, R. G. & Ward Perkins, J. B. (1953). The Roman and Byzantine defences of Lepcis Magna. *Pap. Brit. School, Rome* **21**, 42–74.

Gosselin, M. (1941). *L'hydraulique en Tunisie*. Tunis.

Gregory, J. W. (1911). The geology of Cyrenaica. *Quart. J. Geol. Soc. Lond.* **67**, 576–615.

Gsell, S. (1902). Enquête administrative sur les travaux hydrauliques anciens en Algérie. *Nouv. Arch. Miss. sci. litt.* **12**, Paris.

Guide Bleu (1962). *Grèce*. Paris.

Gunther, A. E. (1964). Re-drawing the coast line of southern Italy: a survey of shifting sea-levels from Gaeta to Malta, with reference to Paestum. *Ill. Lond. News*, **244**, 86–9 (Archaeological section 2167).

Guy, P. L. O. (1958). Archaeological evidence of soil erosion and sedimentation in Wadi Musrara. *Israel Explor. J.* **4**, 77–87.

Happ, S. C., Rittenhouse, G. & Dobson, G. C. (1940). Some principles of accelerated stream and valley sedimentation. *U.S. Dept. Agric. Tech. Bull.* **695**.

Harding, G. L. (1960). *The Antiquities of Jordan*. London.

Harroy, J.-P. (1949). *Afrique terre qui meurt*. Brussels.

Hayes, W. C. (1964). Most ancient Egypt. *Jour. Near Eastern Studies (Chicago)* **23**, 73–114.

Haynes, D. E. L. (1955). *The antiquities of Tripolitania*. Tripoli.

Haywood, R. M. (1937). Roman Africa, *in* T. Frank (ed.) (1933–40), *An economic survey of ancient Rome*. Baltimore. (6 vols.)

Hecht, F., Fürst, M. & Klitzsch, E. (1964). Zur Geologie von Libyen. *Geol. Rdsch.* **53**, 413–70.

Heichelheim, F. M. (1956). Effects of classical antiquity on the land, *in* W. L. Thomas (ed.) (1956), *Man's role in changing the face of the earth*. Chicago, pp. 165–82.

REFERENCES

Heichelheim, F. M. (1958). *An ancient economic history*, 1 (tr. by J. Stevens). Leiden.

Hernández-Pacheco, E. (1928). Les terrasses fluviales de l'Espagne (résumé), *in* K. Sandford (ed.) (1928). *First Report Comm. Plio. Pleisto. Terr.* Oxford, pp. 43–52.

Hernández-Pacheco, E. (1932). *Síntesis fisiográfica y geológica de España*. Madrid.

Herschel, C. (1899). *Frontinus and the water supply of the city of Rome*. Boston.

Hey, R. W. (1956). The geomorphology and tectonics of the Gebel Akhdar (Cyrenaica). *Geol. Mag.* **93**, 1–14.

Hey, R. W. (1962). The Quaternary and Palaeolithic of Northern Libya. *Quaternaria* **6**, 435–49.

Higgs, E. S. (1961). Some Pleistocene faunas of the Mediterranean coastal areas. *Proc. Prehist. Soc.* **27**, 144–54.

Higgs, E. S. & Vita-Finzi, C. (1966). The climate, environment and industries of Stone-Age Greece: Part II. *Proc. Prehist. Soc.* **32**, 1–29.

Highet, G. (1959). *Poets in a landscape*. London.

Higueras, A. (1961). *El alto Guadalquivir*. Zaragoza.

Hilly, J. (1962). Étude géologique du Massif de l'Edough et du Cap de Fer (Est-Constantinois). *Bull. Serv. Carte géol. Alger (n.s.)*, no. 19.

Horton, R. E. (1945). Erosional development of streams and their drainage basins: hydrophysical approach to quantitative morphology. *Bull. geol. Soc. Amer.* **56**, 275–370.

Houston, J. M. (1964). *The western Mediterranean world*. London.

Hubert, J. M. (1948). Glacis d'érosion et sous-écoulement. *Bull. Ass. Géogr. franç.* no. 192–3, pp. 55–61.

Huntington, E. (1907). *The pulse of Asia*. Boston.

Huntington, E. (1910). The burial of Olympia. *Geogr. J.* **36**, 657–86.

Huntington, E. (1911). *Palestine and its transformation*. London.

Huntington, E. (1919). *World-power and evolution*. New Haven.

Huntington, E. & Visher, S. S. (1922). *Climatic changes: their nature and causes*. New Haven.

Ionides, M. G. (1939). *Report on the water resources of Transjordan and their development*. London.

Joly, F. (1962). Études sur le relief du sud-est marocain. *Trav. Inst. scient. chérif., Sér. géologie et géographie physique*, no. 10. Rabat.

Josephus (1959). *The Jewish war* (tr. G. A. Williamson). London.

Judson, S. (1963*a*). Erosion and deposition of Italian stream valleys during historic time. *Science* **140**, 898–9.

Judson, S. (1963*b*). Stream changes during historic time in east-central Sicily. *Amer. J. Arch.* **67**, 287–9.

Julien, Ch. A. (1951). *Histoire de l'Afrique du Nord*. Paris.

La Blanchère, M.-R. du C. (1897). L'aménagement de l'eau et l'installation rurale dans l'Afrique ancienne. *Nouv. Arch. Miss. sci. litt.* **7**. Paris.

Lamb, H. H. (1963). On the nature of certain climatic epochs which differed from the modern (1900–39) normal, *in Changes of Climate*. UNESCO, Arid Zone Research XX, Paris, 125–50.

Lamb, H. H. (1964). The role of atmosphere and oceans in relation to climatic changes and the growth of ice sheets on land, *in* A. E. M. Nairn (ed.) (1964), *Problems in Palaeoclimatology*. London, pp. 332–48.

Lamb, H. H. (1965). The early medieval warm epoch and its sequel. *Palaeogeography, Palaeoclimatol., Palaeoecol.*, 1, *Amsterdam*, pp. 13–37.

Langbein, W. B. & Schumm, S. A. (1958). Yield of sediment in relation to mean annual precipitation. *Trans. Amer. geophys. Un.* **39**, 1076–84.

Lassus, J. (1959). L'archéologie algérienne en 1958. *Libyca. Série archéol. epigr.* **7**, 223–346.

Le Coz, J. (1960). Banasa: contribution à l'étude des alluvions 'rharbiennes'. *Bull. d'arch. marocaine* **4**, 469–70.

Leo Africanus (1956). *Description de l'Afrique* (tr. by A. Épaulard). Paris. (2 vols.)

Leopold, L. B. (1951). Rainfall frequency: an aspect of climatic variation. *Trans. Amer. geophys. Un.* **32**, 347–57.

Leopold, L. B. & Miller, J. P. (1954). A postglacial chronology for some alluvial valleys in Wyoming. *U.S. Geol. Survey Water-Supply Paper 1261.* Washington.

Leopold, L. B. & Miller, J. P. (1956). Ephemeral streams—Hydraulic factors and their relation to the drainage net. *U.S. Geol. Survey Prof. Paper 282* A. Washington.

Leopold, L. B., Wolman, M. G. & Miller, J. P. (1964). *Fluvial processes in geomorphology.* San Francisco and London.

Leroi-Gourhan, A. (1963). Remarques au sujet des températures würmiennes. *Bull. Soc. géol. Fr.* (7) **5**, 414–18.

Le Roy Ladurie, E. (1965). Le climat des XIe et XVIe siècles: séries comparées. *Annales. Économies, sociétés, civilisatio̷* **20**, 899–922.

Lexique (1960). *Lexique stratigraphique international,* vol. IV (*Afrique*), fasc. IVa (*Libye*). Paris, Centre Nat. Rech. Scient.

Lipparini, T. (1940). Tettonica e geomorfologia della Tripolitania. *Boll. Soc. geol. ital.* **59**, 221–301˙

Lombard, M. (1959). Le bois dans la méditerranée musulmane. *Annales. Économies, sociétés, civilisations* **14**, 234–54.

Losacco, U. (1962). Variazioni di corso dell'Arno e dei suoi affluenti nella pianura fiorentina. *Universo, Firenze,* pp. 557–74 and 673–86.

Loup, J. (1960). L'Oum-er-Rbia. *Trav. Inst. scient. chérif., Sér. géologie et géographie physique,* no. 9. Rabat.

Lyell, C. (1872). *Principles of geology* (11th ed.). London. (2 vols.)

McBurney, C. B. M. (1960). *The stone age of northern Africa.* London.

McBurney, C. B. M. & Hey, R. W. (1955). *Prehistory and Pleistocene geology in Cyrenaican Libya.* Cambridge.

McDougall, T. (1956). *Climate in Roman times* (unpublished Ph.D. thesis). London.

Magnier, P. (1963). Étude stratigraphique dans le Gebel Nefousa et le Gebel Garian (Tripolitanie, Libye). *Bull. Soc. géol. Fr.* (7) **5**, 89–94.

Marçais, G. (1946). *La berbérie musulmane et l'orient au moyen âge.* Paris.

Marcet-Riba, J. (1956). Las formaciones cuaternarias de la región costera del Nordeste de España. *Actes Congr. Int. Quatern. IV Rome* (1953), pp. 631–7.

Marchetti, M. (1938). *Idrologia cirenaica.* Florence.

Margat, J. (1962). Mémoire explicatif de la carte hydrogéologique au 1/50000 de la plaine du Tafilalt. *Notes Mém. Serv. Mines Carte géol. Maroc,* no. 150 bis, Rabat.

Marinelli, O. (1926). Sull'età dei delta dei fiumi italiani. *La Geogr.* **14**, 21–9.

Marsh, G. B. (1874). *Man and Nature.* London. (rev. ed.)

Marshall, W. E. (1958). *Annual Report of the Department of Forests for the year 1956–7.* Tripoli.

Marshall, W. E. (1959). *Annual report of the Department of Forests for the year 1957–8.* Tripoli.

Marshall, W. E. (1960). Forestry in Tripolitania, *in* S. G. Willimott & J. I. Clarke (eds.) (1960), *Field studies in Libya.* Durham, pp. 101–110.

Marthelot, P. (1957). L'érosion dans la montagne Kroumir. *Rev. Géogr. alp.* **45**, 273–87.

Martin, P. S. (1963). *The last 10,000 years.* Tucson.

Meiggs, R. (1960). *Roman Ostia.* Oxford.

Mensching, H. (1951). Une accumulation post-glaciaire provoquée par des défrichements. *Rev. Géom. Dyn.* **2**, 145–56.

Mensching, H. (1958). Soil erosion and formation of Haugh-loam in Germany. *Ass. Int. Hydrol. Scient.* (*Toronto*), **1**, 174–8.

Merighi, A. (1940). *La Tripolitania antica.* Verbania. (2 vols.)

Mistardis, G. (1950). Les pédiments arides et semi-arides de l'Attique centrale. *C.R. Cong. Internat. Géog. 1949* (*Lisbon*) **2**, 137–48.

REFERENCES

Monod, Th. (1958). Parts respectives de l'homme et des phénomènes naturels dans la dégradation du paysage et le déclin des civilisations à travers le monde méditerranéen *lato sensu* avec les déserts ou semi-déserts adjacents, au cours de derniers millénaires. *Un. Int. cons. Nat.* **7**. Athens.

Morandini and others (1962). *L'erosione del suolo in Italia*, II. Cons. Naz. Ric., Padua.

Moseley, F. (1965). Plateau calcrete, calcreted gravels, cemented dunes and related deposits of the Maalegh–Bomba region of Libya. *Z. Geomorph.* **9**, 167–85.

Murray, G. W. (1955). Water from the desert: some ancient Egyptian achievements. *Geogr. J.* **121**, 171–8.

Myres, J. L. (1910), *in* E. Huntington, The burial of Olympia. *Geogr. J.* **36**, pp. 679–80.

Myres, J. L. (1953). *Geographical history in Greek lands.* Oxford.

Neuville, R. & Ruhlmann, A. (1941). La place du paléolithique ancien dans le quaternaire marocain. *Inst. des Hautes-Études marocains* VII (École superieure de langue arabe). Casablanca.

Neyrpic (1959). *Station d'étude de l'érosion de Sidi Tabet.* Tunis.

Nossin, J. J. (1959). *Geomorphological aspects of the Pisuerga drainage area in the Cantabrian Mountains (Spain).* Leiden, Ijdo.

Oakley, K. P. (1964). *Frameworks for dating fossil man.* London.

Oates, D. (1953). The Tripolitanian Gebel: settlement of the Roman period around Gasr ed-Dauun. *Pap. Brit. School, Rome* **21**, 81–117.

Oates, D. (1954). Ancient settlement in the Tripolitanian Gebel, II: The Berber Period. *Pap. Brit. School, Rome* **22**, 91–117.

Olausson, E. (1965). Evidence of climatic changes in North Atlantic deep-sea cores. *Progress in Oceanography* **3**, 221–52.

Oldfield, F. (1963). Pollen analysis and man's role in the ecological history of the south-east Lake District. *Geogr. Annlr* **45**, 23–40.

Ortolani, M. & Alfieri, N. (1947). Deviazioni di fiumi piceni in epoca storica. *Riv. geogr. ital.* **54**, 2–16.

Paraskevaidis, I. (1956). Observations sur le Quaternaire de la Grèce. *Actes Congr. Int. Quatern.* IV *Rome* (1953), pp. 167–78.

Parker, F. L. (1958). Eastern Mediterranean foraminifera. *Reports of the Swedish Deep Sea Expedition 1947–8* **8**: Sediment cores from the Mediterranean Sea and the Red Sea, pp. 217–83.

Parona, C. F. (ed.) (1913). *La Tripolitania settentrionale.* Rome. (2 vols.)

Pausanias (1897). *Description of Greece* (tr. J. G. Fraser). London.

Peterson, H. V. & Hadley, R. F. (1961). Effectiveness of erosion-abatement practices on semiarid rangelands in western United States. *Assoc. Internat. Hydrol. Scient., Helsinki*, **53**, 189.

Petrie, Sir F. (1928). Changes of level on the Palestine coast, *in* K. Sandford (ed.), *First Report Comm. Plio. Pleisto. Terr.* Oxford, p. 16.

Pettijohn, F. J. (1957). *Sedimentary rocks.* (2nd ed.) New York.

Philby, H. St J. (1957). *The land of Midian.* London.

Philippson, A. (1950–9). *Die Griechischen Landschaften.* Frankfurt. (4 vols.)

Picard, L. (1932). Zur Geologie des mittleren Jordantales. *Deutscher Palästina Ver. Zeitschr.* **55**, 169–237.

Picard, L. (1938). Synopsis of stratigraphic terms in Palestine geology. *Bull. geol. Dept. Hebrew Univ.* **2**, no. 2.

Picard, L. (1943). Structure and evolution of Palestine. *Bull. geol. Dept. Hebrew Univ.* **4**, nos. 2, 3 and 4.

Picardi, S. (1956). Variazioni storiche del corso dell'Arno. *Riv. geogr. ital.* **63**, 15–34.

Pouquet, J. (1952). *Les monts du Tessala.* Paris.

Pujos, A. (1958–9). Présentation de la carte des sols du Rharb à l'échelle de 1/100,000e par P. Divoux. *Soc. sci. nat. du Maroc, Section de pédologie. Travaux*, pp. 13–14.

Quennell, A. M. (1958). The structural and geomorphic evolution of the Dead Sea Rift. *Quart. Jl geol. Soc. Lond.* **114**, 1–24.

Raikes, R. L. (1967). *Water, weather and prehistory.* London.

REFERENCES

Rainaud, A. (1894). *Quid de natura et fructibus Cyrenaicae Pentapolis antiqua monumenta cum recentioribus collata nobis tradiderunt.* Paris.

Raynal, R. (1961). *Plaines et piedmonts du bassin de la Moulouya (Maroc oriental).* Rabat.

Reifenberg, A. (1953). The struggle between the 'Desert and the Sown'. *Desert Research*, pp. 378–91. Jerusalem.

Reynolds, J. & Ward Perkins, J. P. (1952). *Inscriptions of Roman Tripolitania* (I.R.T.). London.

Ribeira-Faig, J. M. (1950). The Plio-Pleistocene boundary in the north-eastern coast of Spain. *XVIII Int. Geol. Cong. 1948, Sec. H, Part* IX, London, pp. 78–84.

Robaux, A. & Choubert, G. (undated *a*). *Feuille de Foum Tatahouine.* Carte géologique et hydrogéologique provisoire de la Tunisie. Tunis.

Robaux, A. & Choubert, G. (undated *b*). *Feuille de Medenine.* Carte géologique et hydrogéologique provisoire de la Tunisie. Tunis.

Robaux, A., Choubert, G. and others (undated). *Feuilles de Dehibat et Djeneien.* Carte géologique et hydrogéologique provisoire de la Tunisie. Tunis.

Roger, J. (ed.) (1962). Buffon. Les Époques de la nature. *Mém. Mus. natn. Hist. nat., Paris* **10**, I–CLII and 1–343.

Rognon, P. (1962). Observations nouvelles sur le Quaternaire du Hoggar. *Trav. Inst. Rech. sahar.* **21**, 57–80.

Rognon, P. (1967). Climatic influences on the African Hoggar during the Quaternary, based on geomorphologic observations. *Ann. Ass. Amer. Geogr.* **57**, 115–27.

Romanelli, P. (1925). *Leptis Magna.* Rome.

Rostovtseff, M. (1957). *The social and economic history of the Roman Empire.* Revised by P. M. Fraser. Oxford. (2 vols.)

Rowland, J. W. (1945). *Survey of land resources in Tripolitania.* Tripoli.

Schattner, I. (1962). *The lower Jordan valley.* Jerusalem.

Scheidegger, A. E. (1961). *Theoretical geomorphology.* Berlin.

Schulten, A. (1955). *Iberische Landeskunde.* Bd 1. Strasbourg.

Semple, E. C. (1919). Climatic and geographic influences on ancient Mediterranean forests and the lumber trade. *Ann. Ass. Amer. Geogr.* **9**, 13–37.

Semple, E. C. (1931). *The geography of the Mediterranean region.* New York.

Selli, R. (1962). Le Quaternaire marin du versant Adriatique Ionien de la péninsule italienne. *Quaternaria* **6**, 391–413.

Shackleton, N. (1967). Oxygen isotope analyses and Pleistocene temperatures re-assessed. *Nature, Lond.* **215**, 15–17.

Shanan, L., Tadmor, N. H. & Evenari, M. (1961). The ancient desert agriculture of the Negev. VII: Exploitation of runoff from large watersheds. *Ktavim* **11**, 9–31.

Sherwin-Whyte, A. N. (1949). Review of Cary (1949). *J. Roman Stud.* **39**, 162–3.

Smith, G. A. (1894). *The historical geography of the Holy Land.* London.

Sogreah (1959). *Essai de codification des facteurs de l'érosion en Tunisie.* Tunis.

Solé Sabaris, L. (1962). Le Quaternaire marin des Baléares et ses rapports avec les côtes méditerranéennes de la Péninsule Ibérique. *Quaternaria* **6**, 309–42.

Solé Sabaris, L. and others (1952 and 1954). *España, Geografía Física.* vols. I and II of Manuel de Terán, *Geografía de España y Portugal.* Barcelona.

Stella, A. (1914). Geologia, *in* L. Franchetti (1914), *La Missione Franchetti in Tripolitania: (Il Gebel).* Florence, pp. 89–126.

Stewart, J. H. (1956). *A study of Wadi Megenin floods.* U.S.O.M. (U.S. Operations Mission to Libya.) Tripoli.

Stewart, J. H. (1960). *Land and water resources of Tripolitania: a measurement of the land and its potential.* U.S.O.M. Tripoli.

REFERENCES

Tevere (1954). *Rilievi dell'alveo dei corsi d'acqua: Tevere da Ponte Felice a Roma (Ponte Milvio)*. Serv. Idrog. Publ. 23, Fasc. 1, Rome.

Tixeront, J. (1951).Conditions historiques de l'érosion en Tunisie. *Assoc. Internat. Hydrol. Scient.*, Brussels **2**, 73–81.

Toniolo, A. (1950). I regimi dei corsi d'acqua della penisola italiana. *C.R. Int. geog. Cong.*, Lisbon *1949* **2**, 435–54.

Tozer, H. F. (1897). *A history of ancient geography*. Cambridge.

Trabut, L. (1889). *Étude sur l'halfa ('Stipa tenacissima')*. Algiers.

Tricart, J. (1953). La géomorphologie et les hommes. *Rev. Géom. Dyn.* **4**, 153–6.

Trotter, A. (1915). *Flora economica della Libia*. Rome.

Underhill, R. W. (1967). Dead Sea levels and the P.E.F. mark. *Palestine Expl. Q.* **99**, 45–53.

UNESCO-FAO (1963). *Bioclimatic map of the Mediterranean zone (Explanatory notes)*. UNESCO Arid Zone Research XXI, Paris.

Van Bath, B. H. S. (1963). *The agrarian history of western Europe* A.D. *500–1850*. London.

Van Houten, F. B. (1961). Climatic significance of red beds, *in* A. E. M. Nairn (ed.), *Descriptive palaeoclimatology*. London, pp. 89–139.

Van Liere, W. J. (1960–1). Observations on the Quaternary of Syria. *Rijksdienst oudheidk. Podemonderz.* **10–11**, 7–69.

Vaufrey, R. (1934). Les plissements acheuleo-moustériens des alluvions de Gafsa. *Rev. Géogr. phys.* **7**, 299–322.

Vaufrey, R. (1955). *Préhistoire de l'Afrique I: Maghreb*. Paris.

Vinassa de Regny, P. (1912). Cenni geologici sulla Libia italiana. *Boll. Soc. afr. Ital.* **31**, 6–38.

Vita-Finzi, C. (1960*a*). Post-Roman erosion and deposition in the wadis of Tripolitania. *Assoc. Internat. Hydrol. Scient.*, Helsinki **53**, 61–4.

Vita-Finzi, C. (1960*b*). Post-Roman changes in Wadi Lebda, *in* S. G. Willimott & J. I. Clarke (eds.) (1960), *Field studies in Libya*. Durham, pp. 46–51.

Vita-Finzi, C. (1961). Roman dams in Tripolitania. *Antiquity* **35**, 14–20.

Vita-Finzi, C. (1963). Carbon-14 dating of medieval alluvium in Libya. *Nature, Lond.* **198**, 880.

Vita-Finzi, C. (1964). Observations on the late Quaternary of Jordan. *Palestine Expl. Q.* **95**, 19–33.

Vita-Finzi, C. (1966*a*). The new Elysian Fields. *Amer. J. Arch.* **70**, 175–8.

Vita-Finzi, C. (1966*b*). Historical marine levels in Italy. *Nature, Lond.* **209**, 906.

Vita-Finzi, C. (1966*c*). The Hasa Formation. *Man* (n.s.) **1**, 386–90.

Vita-Finzi, C. (1967). Late Quaternary alluvial chronology of northern Algeria. *Man* (n.s.) **2**, 205–15.

Vita-Finzi, C. & Brogan, O. (1967). Roman dams on the Wadi Megenin. *Libya Antiqua*, **2**, 65–71.

Von Hoff, K. E. A. (1822–41). *Geschichte der durch Überlieferung nachgewiesenen natürlichen Veränderungen der Erdoberfläche*. Gotha. (5 vols.)

Ward Perkins, J. B. (1962). Etruscan towns, Roman roads and medieval villages: the historical geography of southern Etruria. *Geogr. J.* **128**, 389–405.

Warmington, B. H. (1954). *The North African provinces from Diocletian to the Vandal Conquest*. Cambridge.

Wilbert, J. (1961). Le Quaternaire dans les Doukkala. *Notes Marocaines (Soc. Géogr. Maroc.)*, no. 16, 5–30.

Willimott, S. G. (1960). Soils of the Gefara, *in* S. G. Willimott & J. I. Clarke (eds.) (1960), *Field studies in Libya*. Durham, pp. 26–45.

Willimott, S. G. & Clarke, J. I. (eds.) (1960). *Field studies in Libya*. Durham.

Woolley, C. L. & Lawrence, T. E. (1960). *The wilderness of Zin*. London.

Zak, I. & Freund, R. (1966). Recent strike slip movements along the Dead Sea Rift. *Israel J. Earth-Sci.* **15**, 33–7.

Zeuner, F. E. (1959). *The Pleistocene period*. (2nd ed.) London.

131

1　The Gebel front and terraces in Wadi Milga.

2　A breach in the wadi calcrete (arrowed). The wadi flows in the direction of the arrow.

3 The two terraces in Wadi Gan E of Tarhuna: (A) upper, (B) lower terrace.

4 The two terraces at the head of Wadi Tareglat (Wadi Tmarmura):
(A) upper, (B) lower terrace.

5   The younger fill in Wadi Turgut. The book is 20 cm long.

6   Dam masonry (D) resting on wadi calcrete (C).

7   Wadi Lebda: dam III (D) perched above wadi (W) which has shifted down calcrete (C). The upper terrace (UT) is being gullied. Fragments of Roman dam (f) litter the wadi bed.

8   Wadi Lebda: dam II (II) and the 'nose' of alluvium (A) deposited by the wadi when it flowed at a higher level (cf. Fig. 16).

9   Alluvium (F) accumulated by a dam in Wadi Ganima.

10   Bedded fill behind dam VIII, Wadi Ganima (cf. Fig. 14).

11 Calcrete in bed of Wadi Megenin being gullied. Modern cistern (c) in background.

12 Wadi Caam in flood near the coast road (cf. Fig. 8). Figure stands on aqueduct
intake; water pours over edge of calcrete, and saps at reservoir (?) wall on left.

13　Wadi Megenin: dams I and II resting on calcrete (C) which has been breached.

14　Lower terrace (T) within channel cut below calcrete (C; note figure) on which
rests a Roman dam (D) in Wadi Umm El Gerfan (Lebda).

15 Wadi Lebda: headwall of breach in calcrete. The white goat stands on the valley floor; upper terrace in background.

16 Gullying of the older fill, Tripolitania.

17 Gullying of floor of Wadi Migdal; Senam Migdal on left.

18 Wadi walls buried by alluvium in Wadi Migdal (trowel on left for scale).

19   One of the surviving *Batoom* trees on alluvial fill sectioned by gully
(Wadi Migdal).

20　Wadi Kuf: post-Classical terrace.

21　Wadi Kuf: general view showing terraces here composed largely of terra rossa.

22   Historical fill (F) resting on eroded tufa (T) at 'Ain Susa.

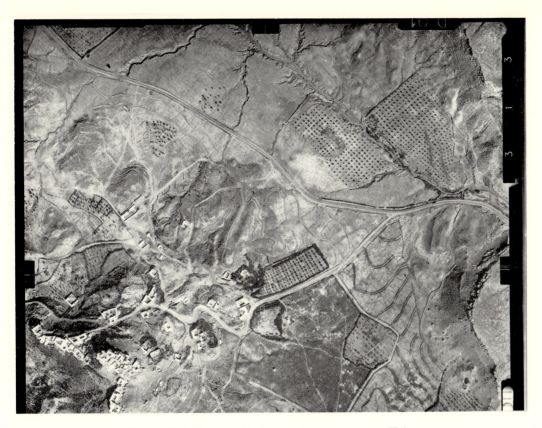

23 The gullied fill and soil-conservation terraces near Takrouna.

24   The lower terrace in Wadi Soummam.

25   The lower (L) and upper (U) terraces in the middle Bou Douaou.

26 The lower terrace (T) in Wadi Deheb.

27 Rharbian terrace in Wadi Sebou.

28 Ruins of Banasa excavated from historical fill. Terrace in distance.

29 Historical fill terrace (T) in Wadi Tensift.

30 Historical fill in Wadi Tamrakht.

31 Gullied fill near Sigilmasa (Rissani).

32   Historical deposit filling a channel cut in older alluvia. Wadi Ziz at Erfoud
(cf. Fig. 31d).

33   The historical fill in the Guadalquivir at Alcalá (cf. Fig. 33d).

34   The historical deposit (right) at Toledo.

35   The Pesa river incised into the historical deposit.

36 The historical deposit in the Arbia, southeast of Siena, after the floods of
November 1966.

37   The ruins of Olympia being excavated from the historical fill (1930).
(Photograph by courtesy of the German Institute of Archaeology, Athens.)

38 The terraced fill west of Selianitika, on the northern coast of the Peloponnese.

39 Extensive historical deposit in a tributary of the Evinos.

40   Wadi Nu'eima: historical fill (H) and Lisan series (L).

41   The historical terrace (T) at Petra, Wadi Musa.

42 At the junction between wadis Rama and Kofrein. Figure stands on upper terrace; lower terrace in foreground.

43 Wadi Er Ruabi: the two terraces.

INDEX

Throughout, *Wadi* is used for *Uadi*, *Oued*, etc., and *River* for *Río*, *Fiume*, etc.

INDEX